# Wisdom
## CALLS OUT TO YOU
What you know can change everything

**Norman Morea Trent Sabadi**

# WISDOM CALLS OUT TO YOU

"WHAT YOU KNOW CAN CHANGE EVERYTHING!"

- Discover the powerful keys of the Wisdom of God and unlock the abundance of Heaven for you today
- Tap into the greatness within you and become a Mighty vessel of healing and blessing for a World in need
- Uncover the masks of Unforgiveness and Pride and set yourself free

*Norman Morea Trent Sabadi*

Copyright © 2017 Norman Morea Trent Sabadi

Second Edition by Norman Sabadi Publishing. Copyright © Norman Morea Trent Sabadi, 2023.

All rights reserved. This book or parts thereof may not be reproduced in any form. No part of this publication may be reproduced, stored in a retrieval system or transmitted in any form or by any means, electronic, mechanical, photocopying, recording or otherwise, without the prior written permission of the publisher. Except for brief quotations on social media or for reviews.
Unless otherwise noted, Scripture quotations are taken from the *King James Version* of the Holy Bible.

ISBN: 978-0-6481142-2-2 (Paperback)
ISBN: 978-0-9756110-4-3 (Epub/Kindle)

Initial Cover Design by Faith Builders International, 2018
Updated Cover Design by Norman Sabadi Publishing, 2023

First Edition. Published by Faith Builders International PO Box 3554, Robina Q 4230, Australia
Second Edition by Norman Sabadi Publishing 8 Allen Rd, Gracemere QLD 4702, Australia

Dedicated to my beloved Mum and Dad with love, from your dear son, Norman

# ACKNOWLEDGEMENT

First and foremost, I give thanks to Jesus, My Lord and My Saviour. For all that I am is in Him.

My beloved mum and dad for your wisdom, guidance and love in *Christ* in raising me to be the person I am. Even though I may have failed at some things in life you still held me up high and encouraged me on with your unwavering arms of love. **I learned wisdom through your unfailing love.**

Also, to all my brothers and sisters, thanks for making this life's journey such a joyous one so far. You are the best, all of you.

To my beloved wife Olivia, and kids, Ethan and Jazmina, I am so blessed to have you in my life. I thank God for your love and courage. You are God's precious gift to me. My joy is your joy, my peace is your peace, and my strength is your strength for in Christ we are *ONE*.

My dear sister, Airegi Joan, for helping make this book pleasantly readable for which I am eternally grateful. Your worthy input has surely added to the value of this book.

Gladys Rozario and Julie Wykes-Herbert for your timely reviews; I express my deepest appreciation for your generous and subservient input into what is my first wisdom book.

Lastly, to my Christian family; you know who you are. It has been a joy to walk alongside you all in the journey of faith as God adds to the group daily. I rejoice with you all in that, our *ONE* Hope is fullness of life in Jesus Christ. Stay strong in the LORD. For when the time is ripe, *Christ will complete His Work of Glory in us.*

# CONTENTS

| | |
|---|---|
| PREFACE | 9 |
| INTRODUCTION | 11 |
| CHAPTER 1 | 21 |
| THE KEYS OF THE KINGDOM: THE POWER OF THE MIND | 21 |
| CHAPTER 2 | 43 |
| THE KEYS OF THE KINGDOM: THE POWER OF THE TONGUE | 43 |
| CHAPTER 3 | 53 |
| THE KEYS OF THE KINGDOM: THE POWER OF PRAISE & PRAYER | 53 |
| CHAPTER 4 | 73 |
| THE VALUE OF THE POWER WITHIN —USE YOUR GIFT | 73 |
| CHAPTER 5 | 103 |
| IT'S ALL ABOUT YOU—YOU ARE PERFECT FOR YOUR SUCCESS | 103 |
| CHAPTER 6 | 117 |
| GREATNESS - VISION - PURPOSE | 117 |
| CHAPTER 7 | 143 |
| THE TRUE POWER OF EXPECTATION | 143 |
| CHAPTER 8 | 147 |
| RAISING A STANDARD AGAINST THE ENEMY | 147 |
| CHAPTER 9 | 161 |
| FORGIVENESS: FIND HEALING FOR YOUR SOUL | 161 |
| CHAPTER 10 | 175 |
| THE POWER OF MEDITATING UPON GOD'S WORD | 175 |
| About the Author | 186 |

# PREFACE

The Voice of the Holy Spirit is calling out to you every second of the day. He is our Comforter who is ever closer to us, much more than we realise. God's desire to be with you is a covenant choice because of His love for you. It is the Heavenly Father looking over your shoulder to point you in the right direction. **God wants you to achieve your dreams, no matter where you are in life.** He calls you to take milk and bread for your soul so that you may discover your life's purpose and walk the full expression of this life in Him (**Isa. 55:1**).

The wisdom in this book was given to me by the Holy Spirit. He is the greatest Teacher ever. He has enabled me to see wisdom in every circumstance. I urge you to respond to the LORD calling out to you today to change your heart and mind and cause a transformation in your life that will raise you to new heights in God. My desire for you is that you be empowered, uplifted, and transformed with a new mindset for success and prosperity in Christ Jesus.

In this book, I am ASKING YOU TO LEARN something that may be old or new to you. The most important lessons that brought you great success were because you had a teachable spirit. The lessons of wisdom that drove you to find your place in life are the ones you gave time to observe. When you got what your heart desired it was because you were teachable enough to learn how to achieve the outcome you wanted. **Be teachable and you will be reachable. Be reachable and you will be formidable (that is, to be extremely impressive in excellence).**

With this, I ask you to begin each chapter with a prayer. After you have read each chapter, I also encourage you to close again with prayer. This is to make concrete what you have received from reading through the leading of the Holy Spirit. Treat wisdom as a precious ornament. Make time to feed your soul and spirit with words of life and you will receive the richness of Wisdom. Digest each page with discovering eyes and a teachable spirit and you will truly experience the overflow of the promises and gifts of God poured out to you through His Wisdom.

To you my readers; May the Holy Spirit rest upon you mightily to direct you in everything you do as you listen to the *Voice of His Wisdom* calling out to you today. May God bring you great success in all that you do because your life is worth more than anything in this world before the eyes of our Loving Father in Heaven.

— **Norman Morea Trent Sabadi**

# INTRODUCTION

## THE SUNDAY SCHOOL LESSON

*"The fear of the LORD [is] the beginning of wisdom: a good understanding have all they that do [His commandments]: His praise endureth for ever."* **Psalms 111:10**

*"The fear of the LORD [is] the beginning of knowledge: [but] fools despise wisdom and instruction."* **Proverbs 1:7**

Many things fascinate me and *Wisdom* is one of them. I always marvelled at *wise sayings*, growing up. The first time I ever understood one with both heart and mind was at the age of twelve years. It was a Mother's Day Sunday Service and during the service, a handful of young university students performed a skit. The message from the skit went something like,

> *"Cherish your mum while she is still here. You may never know one day when you look over your shoulder, you will find her chair empty"*

This left a lasting effect on me. It's been a little over twenty years since then, but I still hear it in my spirit every time I am with my mum and dad. It was also in that same year that I had my first great revelation about God. This time it was a Sunday school message. King David was the subject of discussion. The teacher spoke about how David was *a man after the heart of God*. David earned this place because he praised and worshipped God with all his heart. This intrigued me so much as my young twelve-year-old heart began to understand what it *took* to touch God's heart. After Church, we enjoyed the usual big family lunch. However, I still pondered on the lesson. While eating a brilliant idea came to me. Maybe I should try it, you know — touch the heart of God.

That afternoon, I got on my bicycle and rode around the yard. I had decided while riding my bike, I would sing all the gospel songs, church hymns, praise and worship songs that my young mind could recall. I'd never done anything like this before, so it was already an exciting adventure to embark on.

I began singing my favourite songs first and poured my heart out to Heaven, the best I knew how. My voice rose to God and I sang with joy, sincerity, and intensity. I didn't hold back. I think I started roughly about 2:30 pm and sang until evening came.

I noticed a strange thing began to happen. My heart became lighter, my being saturated with peace and I was covered by a blanket-like tangible feeling. I didn't quite understand it fully but it was a sense of sweet holiness as I think about it now. All I knew was that I was busy reaching out to touch God's heart which gave me great satisfaction. After about four hours later, I felt I had achieved my mission. I didn't exactly know how but my heart overflowed with Heaven's peace and that was a reasonable indicator that I was done. That night as I went to bed sound asleep, a dear friend and sister, Shila was about to do her usual prayers in her bedroom. She opened her Bible to read a passage and then proceeded to say her prayer. She had only begun the opening lines of her prayer when suddenly a bright light entered the room and stairs that reached from Heaven to Earth appeared before her, kind of like Jacob's vision. A mighty angel stood at the base of the stairs and beckoned with his hand for her to join him.

*"The Master awaits you."* Soon they were on their way up the stairs to Heaven. Shila thought to herself about what wonderful things she would see. It seemed only seconds when they reached the top of the stairs. Bright colours of all sorts met her gaze as she entered Heaven's gates. The angel then led her to a room. There the Master was waiting for her. As she entered the room, she recognised who it was.

Shila was in the Presence of Jesus Christ, the Kings of kings, and Lord of all lords and Saviour of the world. Immediately she fell to the floor in reverence before Jesus and worshipped Him. He walked up to her and said,

*"Welcome my daughter. Come quickly now. I have something to show you"* as he helped her to her feet. Shila walked with Jesus through Heaven's beautiful gardens conversing as they went. Jesus then turned to her and asked, *"Can you hear that?"*

It was the sound of children playing in the gardens. They came from a distance and were now running towards Shila and Jesus. The kids came rushing right into Jesus' arms with shouts of excitement and joy. Jesus loved the children; He embraced them and talked with them.

The kids gave Shila hugs too and she enjoyed talking with them. A young lad approached her laughing, smiling and talkative. *"Hey Shila, this is so awesome. It's good to see you here.*

*Isn't Jesus cool?"*

"*Hi Norman, are you here now?*" Shila was surprised and curious all at once, as she observed the appearance of this boy and the striking similarity to someone she knew. "*Could it be him...?*"

The boy hugged her and ran off with the other kids. Shila stood in wonderment. She had just seen me in Heaven with all the other kids. Did I die in my sleep to be amongst them or was she in the same vision with me?

"*It's time to go now, Shila. Did you see? He touched my heart.*" Shila just listened and knew Jesus was talking about me. "*Yes, my Lord.*"

Again, the angel that brought her to Heaven was there to take her back to earth. Jesus hugged her and bid her farewell for now. On their way down, Shila thought about what she had seen and heard. When they reached the bottom of the stairs, suddenly the vision ended and she was back in her room again.

Shila quickly finished the prayer she had started before the heavenly vision. She thanked God for the vision and knew that Jesus wanted her to pass on this message to me unaware that hours before, I had been in pursuit of God's heart.

When morning came, (as was the Monday morning school routine) Shila was up early preparing breakfast for us, the boys. My brothers and I sat to eat and there Shila revealed the vision,
"*I have something to share with you all this morning while you're eating.*" She told the whole story with sincerity and gentleness.

The vision shook me inwardly as she recalled the encounter. My brothers wondered why Shila didn't see them there in

Heaven's gardens, but only me. I wondered why too, yet I knew something more and I didn't think to say it out at the time. I had achieved what David did. I became convinced that anyone could touch God's heart. Unknown to me, I had just become a Christian and the same peace I had experienced hours before flowed out of my heart. I knew something had changed inside of me and it felt special. On the way to school, my brothers asked me why it was that Shila only saw me. It was then that I opened up about the subject — LIKE DAVID, WE CAN TOUCH GOD'S HEART TOO.

While I typed this story, I looked back in time and realised how God has continued to add wisdom to my life over the years. There's no doubt I made my fair share of mistakes and with regret, I learnt those hard lessons. That's perhaps one of the reasons why I am still here and why you're reading this now.

I began writing pieces of this book's material in the year 2004. It started as just a journal of wise sayings to help me in my daily walk. Every day as the Spirit of the LORD spoke to me, the Holy Spirit would unlock wisdom that was new and precious; this newfound knowledge gave me insight to direct my path and also to encourage me during many hard times in my life.

Sometimes the wisdom came at precise moments to rescue me and show me the way forward. I found myself filled with courage and hope on many occasions because this knowledge became my sword and my buckler in every challenge I faced and grounded me with peace when I needed it. Ever since I began, I have not stopped jotting down notes of *Wisdom*.

I discovered that **there is no end to God's Wisdom, that God is Wisdom.** He planted in us the Divine plans and initiatives of wisdom so that we may discover the fullness of our purpose on earth. After many years of putting this journal together, I realised that it was growing into a book and much to my joy, in that, I would be able to share these truths of God's many treasures with the world just like King Solomon did in his time.

**A WORD OF WISDOM TO BEGIN!** I have learnt that when the LORD speaks a specific Word at a specific time, take heed of it and write it down as soon as you can because you are most likely to forget it afterwards. **A Word for the moment could be the Word that can change the course of your life. Catch it before it passes you by so that you don't miss your opportunity to be blessed.**

Hence, this is the approach in which I have taken in putting this book together. With that said, many great men and women have gone before me and have written great pieces. All have had an influence on our lives in some way. Their personal marks of *wisdom* started from the heart and overflowed to the world, imprinted and left in the pages of history to shape our course and give us clues to our destiny. Likewise, in the same Spirit of Wisdom and inspiration, I seek to give you keys for life that will drive you to achieve success and fulfil your God-given purpose in life.

> *"Happy [is] the man [that] findeth wisdom, and the man [that] getteth understanding.* [14] *For the merchandise of it [is] better than the merchandise of silver, and the gain thereof than fine gold.* [15] *She [is] more precious than rubies: and all the things thou can desire are not to be compared unto her.* [16] *Length of days [is] in her right hand; [and] in her left-hand riches and honour.* [17] *Her ways [are] ways of pleasantness, and all her paths [are] peace.* [18] *She [is] a tree of life to them that lay hold upon her: and happy [is everyone] that retaineth her."* **(Prov. 3:13-18)**

INTRODUCTION - The Sunday School Lesson

# CHRIST THE WISDOM OF GOD

*The Voice of Wisdom calling out to you is the voice of purpose. It is also the voice of blessing.*

**(1 Cor. 1:24). The Author of Wisdom is God.** Man's wisdom is vain and empty only seeking to please man and his selfishness but not God **(1 Cor. 3:19-20)**. The foundation and end of wisdom is Christ and all other wisdom that falls short of this is not from God. But God's wisdom is summed up in these words;

*"Trust not in the glory of men because all things are yours, and You are Christ's and Christ is God's."* **(1 Cor. 3:21-23)**

I cling onto hope that rises out of faith, and with exceeding joy I touch the things of faith for your sakes so that your heart may be grounded in the *Wisdom of the Spirit* and not in man. I do this because I know wisdom surpasses all things and endures through many generations for as long as there is life upon this earth, till the LORD declares the end.

**There is no limit to the influence of God. Likewise, there is no limit to the influence of wisdom.** Possess wisdom and you possess true power for life. It is with wisdom that God created the heavens and the earth **(Psa. 104.24)**. Wisdom is close to your heart because it defines *who you are* and *who you want to be*.

**There is honour in finding your true self and there is also honour in living for all that you believe in.** The worth of honour is found deeply embedded in the solid rock of God's wisdom. Do you want wisdom? Then walk in honour and humility toward man and God. If God chose today not to honour the principles by which He created all things you and I would not be here today.

Wisdom is the way of God. It is the code by which God does all things; it reveals the purposes and principles of God. Indeed, **God is a God of purpose and if He says something to you He will make every other purpose bend and submit to fulfil the Word He has spoken to you, only if you will be diligent and faithful to that PROPHETIC WORD.**

This is how the wisdom of God operates; it is God's power in action. **Wisdom can promote you and bring you great success because it is the code to abundance and the master key to life.** Wisdom can prolong your life and protect you from every form of harm. From it, we were created and by it, we live.

You are only able to perceive wisdom from the foundation of humility, truth, honour and faith and this is the only true way given to us to reap the blessings of life and to fulfil our destiny. These virtues will be covered later on in the book.

By God's grace, I am glad to be able to share with you my readers, all that the LORD has planted in my spirit. Let God guide your way because God knows the way. God planted that unique pathway in you so you could find it. **God's wisdom defines the uniqueness of your faith and your perception and thus defines your unique purpose in life.**

If you are willing to make a change today; to start the journey toward transformation and step into your blessings, then I urge you by the Spirit of God to **seek wisdom first and everything else will be added to you (Matt. 6:33).**

I love the revelation of the wisdom of God described by King Solomon, the writer of the Book of **Proverbs**. It's a bit of a read but bear with me because this passage summarises wisdom and lays the foundation for everything else that I talk about in this book. Please read with me;

*"Doth not Wisdom cry? And understanding put forth her voice?* ² *She standeth in the top of high places, by the way in the places of the paths.* ³ *She crieth at the gates, at the entry of the city, at the coming in at the doors.* ⁴ *Unto you, O men, I call; and my voice is to the sons of man.* ⁵ *O ye simple, understand wisdom: and, ye fools, be ye of an understanding heart.* ⁶ *Hear; for I will speak of excellent things; and the opening of my lips shall be right things.*

⁷ *For my mouth shall speak truth; and wickedness is an abomination to my lips.* ⁸ *All the Words of my mouth are in righteousness; there is nothing froward or perverse in them.* ⁹ *They are all plain to him that understandeth, and right to them that find knowledge.*

¹⁰ *Receive my instruction, and not silver; and knowledge rather than choice gold.* ¹¹ *For Wisdom is better than rubies; and all the things that may be desired are not to be compared to it.*

¹² *I Wisdom dwell with prudence, and find out knowledge of witty inventions.* ¹³ *The fear of the LORD is to hate evil:pride, and arrogancy, and the evil way, and the forward mouth, do I hate.* ¹⁴ *Counsel is mine, and sound Wisdom: I am understanding; I have strength.* ¹⁵ *By me kings reign, and princes decree justice.* ¹⁶ *By me princes rule, and nobles, even all the judges of the earth.*

¹⁷ *I love them that love me; and those that seek me early shall find me.* ¹⁸ *Riches and honour are with me; yea, durable riches and righteousness.* ¹⁹ *My fruit is better than gold, yea, than fine gold; and my revenue than choice silver.* ²⁰ *I lead in the way of righteousness, in the midst of the paths of judgment:* ²¹ *That I may cause those that love me to inherit substance; and I will fill their treasures.*

²² *The LORD possessed me in the beginning of His way, before His works of old.* ²³ *I was set up from everlasting, from the beginning, or ever the earth was.* ²⁴ *When there were no depths, I was brought forth;*

*when there were no fountains abounding with water.* <sup>25</sup> *Before the mountains were settled, before the hills was I brought forth:*

<sup>26</sup> *While as yet He had not made the earth, nor the fields, nor the highest part of the dust of the world.* <sup>27</sup> *When He prepared the heavens, I was there: when He set a compass upon the face of the depth:* <sup>28</sup> *When He established the clouds above: when He strengthened the fountains of the deep:* <sup>29</sup> *When He gave to the sea his decree, that the waters should not pass His commandment: when He appointed the foundations of the earth:* <sup>30</sup> *Then I was by Him, as one brought up with Him: and I was daily His delight, rejoicing always before him;*

<sup>31</sup> *Rejoicing in the habitable part of His earth; and my delights were with the sons of men.* <sup>32</sup> *Now therefore hearken unto me, O ye children: for blessed are they that keep my ways.* <sup>33</sup> *Hear instruction, and be wise, and refuse it not.* <sup>34</sup> *Blessed is the man that heareth me, watching daily at my gates, waiting at the posts of my doors.*

<sup>35</sup> *For whoso findeth me findeth life, and shall obtain favour of the LORD.* <sup>36</sup> *But he that sinneth against me wrongeth his own soul: all they that hate me love death."* **(Proverbs. 8:1-36)**

What a masterpiece! This is everything about *Wisdom* and everything about *Christ who is the fullness and glory of God*. He is the Word of life and it is through His Spirit that we are able to unlock the doors of the Kingdom of God.

These doors are ever present before you. You can unlock them by applying understanding to God's Word and by obeying the direction of His Spirit. May the LORD bless you abundantly as you respond in obedience to His wisdom; may He grant you favour and riches found in Him. Be valiant and claim what is rightfully yours today by faith in Jesus, because only true warriors will become conquerors. To God, be all blessing, glory, honour and power forever, Amen!

# CHAPTER 1

# THE KEYS OF THE KINGDOM: THE POWER OF THE MIND

*A man's life does not only consist of the things he outwardly possesses but what is in his heart.* **Luke 12:15**

*Because it doesn't matter how much you have, if you are not sure of your identity you are not sure of your mindset for life.*

**God's Keys are His Words. Hebrews 1:2** says God upholds all things by the *Word of His Power*. Therefore, we understand that His Words are Keys that possess power. In this chapter, including the next few chapters, you will discover those keys and learn how to use them effectively to experience the power of God in your life and fulfil your true purpose and calling in life.

"*And be not conformed to this world: but be ye transformed by the renewing of your mind, that ye may prove what is that good, and acceptable, and perfect, will of God."* (**Rom. 12:2**)

All that affects us directly affects our emotions and thoughts. Every emotion is associated with a thought. Every problem that occurs in life starts with a thought in the mind. Look around you as you read this; everything that surrounds you started with a *thought* either from yours or someone else. When a *thought* is conceived it brings forth an *idea(s)*, which then requires *learning, and planning* (the process and application of knowledge) in order to achieve this idea. *Idea* pursued then *materialises* into what we know today as our world. Yes, our world is literally conceived by the thoughts we have released to create it. This is an established law or principle of wisdom. This process of *thought-producing ideas* which overflow into *reality* is called *The Creative Power* or as we know it, *MINDSET*.

If you can change the perception about your life in your mind then you can change the road you walk on. **To change your life, change your mind first. Your thinking mind will get you somewhere and your believing heart will lead you to that somewhere.** Believing in your vision (or what you focus on) is like fuel behind the fire.

For what is in your mind, when it grows deep roots into your heart, then becomes an addiction or habit and this habit eventually influences everything about you. The Sage English Dictionary & Thesaurus[1] defines *habit* as a pattern of behaviour that is inherited or acquired through frequent repetition. An *addiction is therefore a formed habit,* tenacious in its nature. It is single-minded, steadfast and relentless in its pursuit. Regardless of who you are, everyone will have or has an addiction at different levels. Your addiction is your strongest point of *obsession*. By obsession, I mean your desire, passion, enthusiasm, preoccupation and attraction. **Your addiction or habit is your power to achieve because it is the power behind the drive.**

Don't get me wrong. There are *good* and *bad* addictions. If you are addicted to sex, drugs, and alcohol then you are asserting your power to achieve on the wrong things that will only hurt your life and destroy you. I urge you to seek help and especially help from God because it is God who imparted purpose in you and the passion for your purpose. Did you know, that even depression itself is an addiction? Those with depression fall into the same pit repeatedly even after they have been bailed out many times. The reason for this abuse of power is because **the heart is created to seek purpose and what the heart pursues relentlessly the heart produces.** In the process of seeking purpose, it releases its power of focus on the wrong thing because of lack of wisdom and knowledge, and because of the wrong influence that has forced its weight on the heart causing the heart to submit to its corrupted nature. That is why wisdom is so important in directing the desires of the heart toward one's true purpose.

*"Keep thy heart with all diligence; for out of it are the issues of life."* **(Prov. 4:23)**

Furthermore, to talk about the power of the mind we first need to understand its direct link to the heart. **What affects the heart, affects the mind which then affects everything else around us.** The Bible sums it up perfectly in these words:

*"O LORD God of Abraham, Isaac, and of Israel, our fathers, keep this forever in the <u>imagination</u> <u>of the thoughts of the heart of thy people</u> and prepare their heart unto thee:"* **(1 Chr. 29:18)**

and

> *"But have <u>walked after the imagination of their</u> <u>own heart</u>, and after Baalim, which their fathers taught them:"* (**Jer. 9:14**)

These passages reveal that *thoughts come from the heart*. Seeing this is an established truth, we therefore understand that our lives are shaped by our desires and passions rising for the heart.

You do not have to be a person with advanced knowledge to know if you are hungry or sad or happy and so on. Everything we do in life works around our emotions and thoughts. The *virtues of the Holy Spirit* which are love, hope, faith, mercy, truth, compassion and kindness find their voice in our thoughts and emotions which are then revealed in the subsequent words or actions linked to these thoughts and emotions. We can look at it this way, our thoughts and emotions become a vehicle for the *virtues of God* and are revealed in our actions. Therefore, **our emotions and thoughts in faith-action reveal the virtues of God**. Just as the flesh and sin reveal ungodliness, the fruit of the Spirit (**Gal. 5:22-23**) reveals the righteousness of God. Because we were created with these virtues, we are also able to manifest these virtues uniquely with the diversity planted in us by God. **What we are made of defines who we are**. The true *you* is your inner man; your heart. Desire is found in the deep wells of your heart and can be achieved when you believe and only believe. You can create for the kingdom of righteousness or you can create for the kingdom of the devil and the flesh; what flows out of your heart determines the outcome you receive.

You can either *honour* the LORD GOD by walking in His virtues or you can follow after the devil into a life lost in fear and uncertainty. This truth is so powerful that it has proven itself over and over again in history. Look at the dictators from the past, like the German-Nazi dictator Adolf Hitler; who wanted more than just power and his ambition resulted in World War II that destroyed and devastated millions of lives.

The fact that it took only one man's deep thoughts and intentions which were rooted deep in his heart, coupled with ambitious emotions to achieve his heart's desire shows how much such a truth can change the course of any life and in this example, not only Hitler's life but consequently the lives of millions of others. Hitler had a chronic thought that consumed him and drove his agenda. **If your mind is stayed on what you desire then you have what is called a** *chronic thought.* When you are infected by a chronic thought then maybe the thought is ready to deliver what you have been asking for. So **be careful of the kind of mindset you build; it will affect everything in your life, even the smallest things that you take for granted.**

For those who believe in Christ, we have also been given the mind of Christ (**1 Cor. 2:16**). *The mind of Christ is the ultimate mindset.* It holds God's glory, power and purpose. If you want to walk in this mindset you must first accept God's Words because the keys are found in His Words of righteousness, honour, truth and holiness. God is and has been revealing His heart and mind to us through His Words. If you have ears, listen to what the Spirit of God is saying to you. If *mindset determines the outcome*, then we should want only the mind of Christ because the outcome is the *manifested Glory of God*.

Now this is important. Whatever the mindset you are in right now, you possess the attributes of 'attitude and ambition' to create. **The root of great feats and achievements is found in the ambition behind them.** You could also say it this way; **it is the attitude and the ambition behind the action that determines the outcome. Your attitude determines access. God will only take you as far and high as you are willing to go.**

*'Mindset' is our God-given creative power to achieve anything.* If you want to see your dream become a reality you must own this dream in your heart and mind, and you must want it so bad that it becomes your life.

You can be anything you want if that is what lies in your heart. All it takes is for you to listen to wisdom and wisdom will direct your path. Your mindset also reveals the presence that you carry. **The presence you build around you is what you continuously hold and encourage in your mind.** Build your mind for good things and you will always have good things. **Build your mind for great things and you will walk into great things.** If love is not in your home or relationship anymore it's because you have not allowed it to become your mindset. **Without the presence of love, there is no following of love.** To speak about love is powerful but to demonstrate love is even more powerful. The problem is not the other person; the root of the problem lies in your mindset which has its roots deep within your heart. Remember, your mindset reveals your heart, your ambitions, and the presence you carry to influence others and the situations you are in. **Your mindset holds your power to change, direct and influence.**

If you honour wisdom, then you have common sense and understanding which is grounded in faith and love. This attitude for wisdom will promote you and eventually bring you great success. On the flip side, if you allow an evil thing to grow in you, it will only hinder your progress and cause you frustration. If your mind dwells on hate, unforgiveness and anger you will get more of it heaped on you. **The more evil your heart falls into, the closer you are to destruction.** But if you are consistent with righteous living then you are closer to your miracle and breakthrough. God directs the steps of a righteous person.

If you grumble about something it will do you no good. You gain nothing from your complaining as your whining will not help to solve the problem but only add to it, causing a hindrance to good progress. So stop complaining and put your grudges aside so that you do not hinder the good things that want to enter into your life. **To embrace the good in every situation is to promote progress.** It is better for you to walk in the mindset of hope than to harbour disappointment and failure.

Righteousness will always fill you up with joy and liberate you, but the fleshly nature will only create stress and weigh you down. **Any progress is good progress; doesn't matter if it is big or small.**

As long as you are moving forward that is progress because every step you take gets you closer to your destination. Therefore, if you think being successful is far from you, maybe you need to stop standing still and start walking towards success. *Momentum* is good if you are to see *acceleration* in the progress. It could be that you are perhaps only three inches away from what might be the golden opportunity of a lifetime.

Which brings me to ask you, what is your life's course? Where you are now is a result of your own choices. The decisions you have made both consciously and subconsciously are leading you down the path of either utter destruction or complete victories. The choice is yours! Have you checked your compass of life lately? Are you on the right track? Check your Navigational aid. Navigational aid, you say? By this I mean, your heart. **Your heart should be your indicator of how happy you are in life and thus it shows if you are on the right path to getting all you want.** Are you happy with your current situation? Have you planned your life strategy to achieve your ultimate goal, which is your happiness? What steps have you taken so far to get there? The ultimate question to ask yourself is "WHAT DO YOU WANT?"

I urge you to choose an abundant life. You can choose not to live one more day through that pain, hurt or frustration because you don't have to. Don't leave it till tomorrow because you don't know what tomorrow brings, but you can affect the change in your today and find peace for your soul. **Choose Christ and you choose life. Choose His Words of life and you choose blessing, healing and deliverance.**

Whatever your answer is, I encourage you to go on reading because this book is meant to open your mind and your heart to endless possibilities for success and prosperity found in Christ Jesus, the *Wisdom of God*. As you respond to His Voice calling out to you, I urge you to turn your heart onto the right path toward the LORD GOD of all things. He alone can bring you great success beyond your ability to perceive it. God told me once, **"What I (God) can do supersedes your ability to perceive it."**

You will always make a decision based on what your heart agrees upon. Reasoning has its place in the whole process but it is your heart that passes the final decision and sends this decision to the mind to execute. And if your heart is stayed on Christ then you will experience the fullness of life in Christ.

The daily decisions to get up and go to work and so forth cause us to be in a specific place of our choosing at the time we hope to achieve this.

We make *decisions* every second of our life both consciously and unintentionally and every decision begins in our heart. Decisions to submit and follow, or take control and lead, decisions to solve a problem and decisions to create one. As plain as it sounds our world is created by our own *desires* and *decisions*. That means you can create a world of success and happiness or you can create a world of sorrow and hurt. It's about taking control of your life by making solid decisions that will bring about positive changes that lead to your success and happiness. If you let the bad experiences of life dictate and destroy you, you have no control over your own choices.

> *"He that hath no rule over his own spirit is like a city that is broken down, and without walls."* (**Prov. 25:28**)

Imagine yourself sitting on your couch watching TV and then you felt like you wanted a drink. So you went to check the fridge only to find you've run out of lemonade. So you decide to run down to the shops to grab yourself that lemonade because that's all you want to drink at that moment. While at the shops you bump into an old friend who apparently is also there grocery shopping. So you both pause for a minute to catch up and chat about things happening in your life.

Now let's pause the story there and look at some fundamental truths in it. The word coincidence was given for incidents like this but this is exactly what I'm talking about, the amazing creative power of life. If you hadn't chosen to go down to the shops at the exact same time as him, you wouldn't have run into your friend. But this result came about because of the choices you and that individual made at that precise moment. Hence, for a fact, **everyone in life is where they are because of the choices they have made.**

Are you in the right place right now? If not then don't despair, and don't lose hope. The true warrior is the one who keeps on getting up every time he gets knocked down. **You can never be a conqueror unless you first become a warrior for success.** Make the choice today to walk towards your desired outcome and GO!

Just *GO* towards it without fear or hesitation, just as simple as if you were going to buy yourself that delicious lemonade without thinking any other thought about it. You just do it naturally as you would. You have the power within to make the choice right now to achieve your dream.

**Don't wait for tomorrow to go after success because our tomorrows are shaped by our today.** Choose to speak words of life and blessing for the sake of your future, believe in yourself and the dream that God has planted in your heart and pursue it.

**The more we focus on being a blessing, the deeper the roots of peace and favour grow in us and cause us to become unshakable.** This foundation of blessing is love. There is no fear in perfect love and the love of God is full of peace.

Do you want the pages of your life to be filled with stories of blessings? Then let love be the foundation of your heart. Know that, **no one else can write your story for you, only you can.** We are all different; created by God for different purposes; it is only fitting to say you tell your own story the way God has ordained it. If you are not sure of what story to tell, go to God our Creator who holds the original book of our life's story. Even our future is already written in His books. Once you find your purpose on earth the rest of your story will flow off God's pages into yours because the Creator only intended blessing and prosperity for you. Seek Him and He will give you the wisdom and the peace to succeed in life because that is what He wants for you.

*"...let the LORD be magnified, which hath pleasure in the prosperity of His servant."* (**Psa. 35:27**)

Your *imaginations* are not just images because they come from the heart. The book of Jeremiah speaks a lot about this link using words, and *the imaginations of their heart*. What is knowledge without imagination?

Knowledge speaks 'gravity' but imagination says you can fly. Imagination is the initial platform where knowledge can build upon. **Your imagination is the creative faculty of your mind. It can be inter-changeable with the word, thoughts.**

So the point is that, every thought you think will affect something in your life either in a big or small way, whether you know this or not, accept this truth or not. This is a *key of wisdom* and one you cannot ignore. Before God created the heavens and the earth He used the faculty of imagination to design them first before He actualised and brought them forth *into existence* by the power of His Words.

**So there is already equal power in the thinking process before it is spoken.**

Knowledge is only effective when you activate the faculty of creativity in the mind to use it to then, achieve its purpose. There is no limit to what you can create in your imagination but there is a danger in using this creative power for the wrong things. With imagination, you can be and do anything you want. Look at it this way, **if you can successfully execute a process in the mind, then you are not far from understanding the power of your mind.** That if you can see and keep seeing what you want, it will come to you without failure.

What's the real standard for you then in your mind? It's being the edge for others and the edge for all generations. That is the real standard. **When you set your heart on the will of God there**

**is no greater standard than this.** You are blessed, so you can be a blessing to others. You are rich not only for yourself but for others. So do not compromise yourself by undermining others.

Anything is possible; anything is achievable when you imagine it first. It doesn't matter how big your dream is, it can be achieved if you put your heart into it and stay with it. I was sitting down one day on my balcony and these words came strongly to me, *"To walk a desired path you must create this path in your mind."* And I thought about these words echoing deep within me. If you want to walk the path of prosperity you must first create this path for yourself. To walk any path; rough and narrow or easy and wide, up or down, steep, sloppy or flat, there is always a first step. Are you taking a step toward your path today?

Whatever the path you should walk, know that eventually, you will get there because a pathway always leads somewhere. **A persistent mind for success will reap consistent results which eventually lead to walking a purpose-driven life.**

## FAITH - KNOWLEDGE - WISDOM

*"For My thoughts are not your thoughts, neither are your ways My ways, saith the LORD. ⁹ For as the heavens are higher than the earth, so are My ways higher than your ways, and My thoughts than your thoughts."* **(Isa. 55:8-9)**

Our mind possesses power and this comes from the fact that it possesses knowledge to act. Deriving from this, my focus is the 'how' that enables us to use knowledge; this is true for those who consider themselves to be intelligent, wise and powerful. **What you learn and how well you learn it will determine how well**

**you apply it and what outcome you get from it.** No matter how much you learn if you do not apply it, it becomes useless. Learning is growing not only in knowledge but in understanding and application. **Knowledge doesn't become important or useful to you until you find the purpose and objective that requires this knowledge to be learned and used**.

KNOW WHAT YOU WANT! It's the reason and motivation behind learning that is key to how much you learn and how well you will apply this knowledge. Knowledge is an ocean and you only benefit from what and how much you fish from it. Thus, an experienced fisherman knows how to catch his fish and where to catch it. The 'how' to attain and apply knowledge finds its power from why you learn and, is important. This determines how much you can take in and commit to your heart so that you can apply it effectively when it is needed. If you don't follow the recipe correctly you won't get the result you want, and **the recipe for effective application is effective learning.**

## THE KEYS OF THE KINGDOM.

Learning precedes success. Learning how to succeed is important. Thus, **the purpose of knowledge is this: we understand to apply and we learn towards success.** Knowledge becomes a powerful tool in your hand if you know how to use it well. If you respect knowledge it can elevate you to greater heights of success.

There is one knowledge greater than all knowledge. It is the knowledge of the Glory of God found in the face of Christ (Eph. 1:16-23). The pursuit of this God-knowledge is the ultimate pursuit of life. **The ultimate pursuit of purpose then is to seek after Christ, the fullness of God (Eph. 3:19).**

With that said, also know that every form of knowledge given to us by God is relevant for our walk in life. **The path to prosperity and great success is the path of *diligence toward knowledge and understanding*.** A lack of knowledge and understanding is a decline in moral standards. By *moral standards* I mean, respect, honour, truth, integrity and love.

To respect others is to respect the wisdom with which the LORD created them. To love others is to love the LORD who created them for we are all uniquely and wonderfully made for the glory of God. So **the place of peace, respect and blessing is the place of high moral standards because the value of anything depends on the standards upheld for it. Therefore, your value is equal to the standards you uphold.**

*Lower your standards and you lower your value.* The price placed on an item depends upon the value that item offers to us. Those who respect, honour and love possess the greatest value: God. *If you value your success then raise the standard of your attitude for it.*

**Success is the result of the level of attitude that produced it. You must have an attitude and appetite for success if you want to be successful in life.** Your success depends on your energy and attitude toward it. High energy means high attraction properties. **Raise the energy of your thinking and belief, and you will attract the right kind of people who will play a big part in achieving your success.** What sets the rich apart from the poor is their attitude towards their success and what they define this success to be. **There is a blueprint for every form of success in life for every endeavour and every path taken.** Find this blueprint and you find your way to success. If you are diligent about success eventually, it will come to you. The power of *intention* makes you look at success differently in that you are willing to do anything to fulfil the purpose of your heart.

*Your willingness to learn* to succeed will teach you to be humble and thankful for the experiences you gain. This will eventually pay off for you in your pursuit of success. Personal success is a result of the right heart-attitude that grooms one for great achievements. From a Christian perspective, a lack of knowledge and faith in God results in a decline in moral standards and a falling away from God's Truth. Without deviating too much from the subject, there is a direct link with upholding high moral standards and wealth. **A nation economically and spiritually crumbles when its moral standards deteriorate.**

**Faith is never without knowledge and the two are inseparable.** You require faith to *discover* knowledge and to *accept* this knowledge once you have *acquired* it. You also require faith to *apply* this knowledge. Faith, like knowledge, is dynamic in nature and is always changing and growing; you go from a *LEARNING-FAITH TO A KNOWING-FAITH.*

Expounding this point, you find *learning* in all stages of the *faith-knowledge* cohesion. We *discover* through observation and learning, *accept* because of learning, *acquire* through learning, *apply* what we have learnt, *grow* when we have learnt and *grow some more* when we continue to learn.

Wisdom, concerning the aforementioned, is the *ability* to discover, acquire, understand and utilise knowledge by the vehicle of faith.

In conclusion, the foundation of knowledge is wisdom. Under the guardianship of wisdom, we experience the true essence of an abundant life. Indeed, it is life and hope for the needy and healing for the wounded heart. To understand the ways of God is life. However, to depart from wisdom is foolishness.

## KNOWLEDGE AND MIND-SET

Why this talk of knowledge? Because *the mindset you have is shaped by the knowledge you possess.* A soldier thinks and lives like a soldier. A medical doctor thinks and lives like one.

And a child of God too should think and live in the mindset of Christ. **Knowledge determines mindset, which determines identity and status and cultivates specific results exclusive only to the knowledge acquired and applied.** The example of specialist jobs such as a trained soldier or a medical doctor shows the truth that those who work in these fields chose to pursue specific knowledge to become who they are in order to achieve a specific purpose in life. With the right kind of knowledge, you have the choice by wisdom to shape the future you want. And if God's wisdom and knowledge are in every decision you make then you can look forward to walking in spiritual abundance with the LORD (**Psa. 23:6**).

Let's solidify this point. **The words we speak and the mindset we carry reveal what door we will unlock.**

**If you've been bitter about things not working for you, you'll keep opening the same doors of disappointment until you change the way you think.** If we set a trained standard in our mind, it is hard to untrain, because the mind also begins to act as a filter, choosing only what is now familiar to it. That is why we have so many prejudiced, narrow-minded people out there who cannot see the light nor understand what it is like to live in the light because they only live in their familiar world full of restrictions, limitations and fears governed by their own rules and not God's.

No matter what your definition of prosperity is, God is still the author of it because He is the author of life and wisdom. He leads you to attain success and wealth, both physically and spiritually in Christ. **What you want and where you want to be are meaningless if God's purpose is not in the picture.** When you look at God's Word, its treasures are only possessed by faith in it. So you cannot come to a deeper knowledge of God and His infinite love and glory until you release the faith in your heart to accept it.

God does not complicate things but He simplifies them for us to understand and apply. Take for example **Matthew 6:33** which says,

> *"Seek ye first the Kingdom of God and His righteousness and all these things shall be added onto you."*

Or how about **Luke 6:38**, which says, *"Give and it shall come back to you, good measures, pressed down, shaken together, running over, shall man give to you. For the measure you set is the measure that will come to you again."*

What is the measure you have set in your mind? That same measure will come back to you. With this, I encourage you to seek after the ultimate mind, Christ (**1 Cor. 2:16**).

# MY DREAM
# THE SUPERNATURAL LIBRARY
# OF THE MIND

I thought I should add some flavour to the topic of the power of the mind by telling you about this dream which I had on the 1st of October 2011.

Our mind is not just an ordinary library that stores our past experiences. No, there's more to it than we know. There is something our mind acquires from birth that is pure in its nature. To discover it is to find hidden wealth. Our minds really are a supernatural library waiting to be tapped. I would like to share this dream with you to make you think deeper about the hidden knowledge that exists and the endless capability and potential our mind possesses.

I had this amazing dream about the *mind*. I was taken into a place in the mind where there was a very huge library. I had never seen one like it before. In the library, there was a *voice*. I recognised it as my own voice and I somehow had this knowledge that I was in my own mind, literally speaking, and that this was the voice of my mind. (I will address him as the voice). To my amazement, the voice spoke to me and said, *"Welcome to the Library of Your Mind."* I went *"WOW! Does this place really exist?"* I was astounded by its enormity and I could not fathom that such a place could really exist. This was not just a huge library of memories. It was more than that and I was about to find out. The *voice* led me to a section in this library where there were books of all sizes and colours categorised into subjects just like any normal library.

I thought to myself, how in the world could I have possibly acquired and stored all this knowledge in here? This is where it gets interesting. Here in this place is knowledge that you acquire both consciously and subconsciously, yes that's right, subconsciously. I learnt here that the knowledge acquired by the subconscious mind is millions, perhaps even billions or trillions of times more than what you could consciously acquire from formal education and by your own life experiences. During one's life, when we rise from sleep to face each new day, we do more than just our daily routine. We are constantly required to make choices in a monotonous or upbeat lifestyle, which may vary with individuals.

When you touch things around you, you make contact with a 'supernatural transfer form of energy'. I call it 'knowledge energy.' This energy is spontaneously and supernaturally transferred to this library in your mind to be stored there by the vehicle of your senses: touch, smell, sight, hearing, taste, and intuition or discernment. Similar to a computer network except that this is the KNOWLEDGE-ENERGY NETWORK. I discovered that you know everything you need to know in every aspect of the word knowledge, without consciously knowing it really exists. How is this possible? Well as I explained, you acquire this knowledge without even perceiving it or partaking in it, as you may think (at the conscious, primitive level). As quantum physics reveals we and all other matter are made of energy, which can neither be created nor destroyed. We through this interaction of energies acquire all of this knowledge supernaturally.

The *voice* showed me books that existed in this library of things I have no knowledge of and would not be able to apply in real conscious life. I was taken to this section where a golden book was opened before me and I was asked to read it. This massive book was readable like any book. I then read books like maths, science, physics, history and many more. I also noticed my ability to comprehend was at a much higher level than when in my conscious mind, it was superhuman-like. How could all these be possible?

The voice then said, "I want to show you this next place. You have got to see it." I was so mesmerised, that I just nodded with excitement and willingly followed.

Then I was carried to this room which had a special see-through wall dividing it, similar to a glass wall but one which you could walk through. All the other rooms had the same layout with the same walls. In this room, there was something different happening. It felt very distinctive maybe because of its function which I was about to discover. I could see numbers and letters floating about in the air constructed in a 'knowledge cloud.' When this huge mass of calculations and formulas combined into a new form, a book appeared in the air to receive the newly invented knowledge.

This book was made specifically for it and when all the information had been supernaturally imprinted into this book it was then stored with many other special books already done up in the same manner from this extraordinary room which I tagged as THE INVENTION ROOM.

While I observed this happening, the voice then said, *"You know all that knowledge that you saw earlier, which is acquired and stored in this library, well it doesn't just sit there. Your mind uses all of this knowledge to create solutions, new programs, new and advanced technologies and inventions that can be used, much of which is still undiscovered. Some of the technologies that you know of have already been discovered and used by man but still there is much more to be discovered and the solutions and references are already made here ready to be released to you for the world. This is the CREATION ZONE of anything and everything. To simply put it, energy knows energy and it can take the shape of anything it chooses and create a balance or construct evolved from energies that already exist in their own form, like a mouldable and lively substance that evolves and creates constantly to fulfil a balance. So **we literally become creators of our own world. What you choose to believe in is what you will** create."

I thought to myself, *"So what now? Wouldn't it be wonderful to use this hidden knowledge and connect to this library through the KNOWLEDGE-ENERGY-NETWORK?"* Imagine if you had access to this library 24/7. You could write countless books, reveal solutions and create new inventions that were once only a dream of the past. You would be hundreds of years ahead of time with newly discovered technologies.

The dream ended and I woke up in deep thought about the supernatural library. I wondered why God would give me such a dream. Could such a place really exist in the mind of every person?

The part that stood out the most to me was the message,

*"What you choose to believe in is what you will create."*

Endnote:
1 Definition of Habit, The Sage English Dictionary & Thesaurus, Sequence Publishing, 16 January 2012

# CHAPTER 2

# THE KEYS OF THE KINGDOM: THE POWER OF THE TONGUE

*"The words of a man's mouth are as deep waters, and the wellspring of wisdom as a flowing brook."* **Proverbs 18:4**

*"A fool's mouth is his destruction, and his lips are the snare of his soul.* [8] *The words of a talebearer are as wounds, and they go down into the innermost parts of the belly."* **Proverbs 18:7-8**

*"A man's belly shall be satisfied with the fruit of his mouth; and with the increase of his lips shall he be filled.* [21] *Death and life are in the power of the tongue: and they that love it shall eat the fruit thereof."* **Proverbs 18:20-21**

I spoke about the power of "thoughts and emotions" and their direct link with the heart. The same truth is found with our tongue. For what the mouth speaks is what the heart is full of. **The key to our blessings lies in our tongue.**

But before we go on any further, I want you to understand first, that every *WORD possesses FUNCTION and PURPOSE. When we seek to know the meaning or definition of a WORD, we are seeking to discover its purpose and function.* Therefore, we identify with a word because it relates to a function and a purpose that we understand or are familiar with. So if I say, 'you are *great*' I am releasing the purpose and function of the word *'great'* on you. And here's the amazing part: the remarkable link between a *word* and a *thought!*

We have established from the previous chapter that mindset or creative power is the process that begins from the heart which becomes a thought that produces ideas that when pursued manifest and become a reality. **The whole creative power process (from thoughts to reality) is never without WORDS. Therefore it is never without function and purpose.** This is the reason why man and his world cannot live by bread alone (a physical result) but by every WORD (function and purpose) that comes from the MOUTH OF GOD.

**The spirit realm deals with words.** In the spirit realm words are substance, they are the code of the spirit realm. That is why Christ Jesus, who is the Word of God and the quickening Spirit, is Lord over all realms of the spirit, called HEAVENLY PLACES. He is the Word of life—so if Christ said man shall not live by bread alone but by every word spoken from the mouth of God that means man's spirit needs Words to survive and live. However, not just any words, words from God the Author and Finisher of man's faith in God. Words flow like rivers and fast like the wind. The spirit realm flows in such a manner, as deep wells within men and only wisdom from God is able to draw it up for man to use. Jesus said if one would believe in Him out of their belly would overflow streams of living waters. Jesus was referring to the overflowing of the Words of Life and Power of the Holy Spirit to take life-giving Words from within the Supernatural of God's own Spirit and overflow them into the natural of man. This means Jesus affects the change of a man who first believes in Christ (making them new and causing their spirits to experience the new birth in Christ). They become new within and are a new creation overtaken by the Words of The Holy Spirit within.

**Bread is to the Body as Words of life are to the spirit of a man.** To correct the error of man Christ spoke into the realm of the spirit where the spirit and soul (reasoning and willpower) live. This effected the change of God upon man by taking authority over the spirit realm through the power of God that rested upon Christ.

IF WE AS PHYSICAL BEINGS EXIST (with function and purpose), that means SPECIFIC WORDS WERE RELEASED TO CREATE US. Our individual lives are like a book full of mystery and power. It is unfolded when the right pieces come together. If the puzzle of life is to be complete, the key to this is found in the power of our *words*.

**A man is as he speaks because a man is as he thinks and both are building blocks of the spirit man. If you want blessing then speak blessing. Our blessings lie in the confessions we make.** If speaking words of life and goodness is not a big deal to you, how then can you say you have wisdom when wisdom is not in your tongue? If you criticise others, what good does it add to you? Some things are better kept a secret than spoken. It is better to hold your tongue rather than say it out and later regret you said it. Remember, what the ear has heard, it has heard.

Don't be entangled with vain conversations.

When you find yourself criticising or judging others this will disrupt the peace in your heart and force on you an unnecessary burden. If you speak godly words then wisdom's light will illuminate your being, and *the pathway before you becomes visible and achievable.*

**You first lay down the path of success by the words you speak because your words are established by the functions and purposes found in your heart.** If you lay down for yourself the path of blessing then it will lead you to your destiny. If you choose to curse then it will draw you away from your path of blessing and lead you back into captivity. Breakthroughs will come but how far are you willing to go for them? God wants to take you all the way passed Jordan and into your promised land. **Jeremiah 29:11** says, God wants to bring about your peace and to give you that expected END, that is what He has in mind for you. If God's intent is that He should not stop till He gets you there then again I ask, how far are you willing to go with the LORD to pursue your destiny of blessing.

**Your diligence will lay down for you the path of blessing and they that cross this path will themselves be blessed.** These words of wisdom are also found in the Words of promise God gave to Abraham,

> *"And I will make of thee a great nation, and I will bless thee, and make thy name great; and thou shalt be a blessing:* [3] *And I will bless them that bless thee, and curse him that curseth thee: and in thee shall all families of the earth be blessed."* **(Gen. 12:2-3)**

This path of diligence is found in your heart but discovered in words and actions. If wisdom is the light of the heart, and the lamp to our feet, then we should think it, and speak it in everything we do.

**Our words begin as seeds, which have the potential to create anything we want. Whether for cursing or for blessing either way you will still eat the fruit of your own words.** Yes, your words, sown as seeds, eventually become fruits. The question is, are they good fruits that are delicious to eat or are they awful-tasting fruits that cause others to avoid the tree itself? In Isaiah 61, the prophet speaks about the Trees of Righteousness, the planting of the LORD. But how can we be trees of righteousness if our words don't speak righteousness? So if you profess to walk in righteousness it should be revealed in your fruits: your words and your actions.

**Every time you speak you are creating in the realm of the spirit. You are either locking or unlocking doors with your confessions and declarations.** What you create by your words affects the realm of the spirit and then flows into the natural in its due time.

**Every blessing that is in your future lies in the words you use to create them.** Your blessings are tangible and the moment you speak them with faith they first become tangible in the spirit and are ready to manifest into the natural. The more you declare them in the natural; you build them like rain clouds in the spirit realm till they are too heavy to contain any more rain that they begin to pour into the natural realm (**Isa. 55:10-11**). Your words are like water. When you pour them into the container of the supernatural they will eventually overflow into the natural. Again, in your own tongue lies your blessing and God is both the originator and instigator of blessing because He alone through wisdom is able to direct us to our destiny. The more you bless the closer you are to your destiny in life.

Words that change lives are words whose price is worth more than gold, silver or any precious gem because our words discover our identity and reveal our purpose, drawn out from wells in our hearts. To be a blessing is a profitable thing. A good heart produces good fruits. But an evil heart produces corrupt fruits. **If you are careless with your tongue it will bite back at you like a snake and its poison may destroy you.**

Life and death are surely in the power of the tongue because every word you say either cleanses and blesses you, or defiles and curses you. **The more filth there is that comes out of your mouth, the thicker the poison that is in you.** Avoid unclean language and shallow talk. No one in their right mind would ask a venomous snake to bite them a hundred times. So then, why would you poison and kill yourself with words that destroy the heart and soul? Do yourself a favour and bless others so that you will receive blessings that will last forever, even unto the third and the fourth generation.

If your words are good and filled with blessing then they are like a tree filled with delicious fruits that satisfy the needy soul; they are like fresh clean water that quenches the thirst and how wonderful it is when pure water overflows in abundance. A house of thieves is a house full of liars; a house riddled with gossip is a house full of strife.

Evil words are from the pits of hell. Hence, **be careful as to what you say, for life and death are in the power of the tongue.** The mouth that speaks evil and lies will have no friends but will instead inherit a bad reputation because no one wants to be friends with a liar. Instability and uncertainty will always follow the lying tongue, and whoever makes friends with him will partake in his destruction. The mouth that speaks evil lays traps for its own soul. Bad conversations are a breeding ground for stress, division and sickness but good conversations promote unity, health and well-being. Bless others with words of life and try to do good to them always. Be fair and honest in your dealings and truthful in your conversations, and you will inherit blessings.

The confessions you make are a bridge between your present and your future. Whatever you channel through this connection will always affect your future.

If you bless in your present then you will meet blessing in your future. What you speak continuously is what you will receive. **The mouth that speaks blessing has a heart that follows God** but the mouth that curses, brings forth evil. Evil only deprives you of your right to inherit blessings. Filthy words only burden the heart and become an obstacle to progress.

**Stop cursing your past because it gives your present an overload of garbage that your future cannot handle.** In other words, if you keep cursing past offenders because of what they did to you, you are soon to fall into the pit of destruction created by your own words.

If it is going to be an overload that will affect your future, then it should be an overflow of blessings. **What doesn't fix the problem only adds to the problem—cursing and worrying never fix any problem.** They are like two troublemakers who only want to gossip about your past in an attempt to fill you up with garbage so that there won't be any space left for blessings to flourish in your future. **If you feed on past hurts you will never be satisfied. Your situation is worse than hunger itself.** This may be one reason why you keep experiencing dryness or bad things in your life perhaps because you are still dwelling on the pain and the hurt. Let it go and begin to speak words of blessing and change the course of your life. Bless your present so that your heart will be filled with joy and strength to take on tomorrow.

The true result that satisfies the heart is the result that comes from blessed words. Jesus said in **Luke 6:27-28; 31, 38**:

> *"Love your neighbour and do good to them who hate you. Bless them that curse you and pray for them which despitefully use you*
> *... And as ye would that men should do to you, do ye also to them likewise ... For with the same measure that ye mete withal it shall be measured to you AGAIN."*

I encourage you to pray for those that hurt you, hate you, or curse you and despitefully use you. Pray that God will bless them and bring them the breakthrough that they need. You ask, why should I pray for the undeserving, selfish, and prideful?

(Read all of **Luke 6** to find out why). When you do this for them in prayer you are actually doing this for yourself. It's a principle of the spirit realm; *words create*. The measure in which you set to them is the same measure used on you to deliver the blessing back to you. Even in prayer, your own mouth will bring forth your blessing and the same mouth will bring forth your cursing.

Do you want blessing? Then bless and the same will be returned to you!

> *"Finally, be ye all of one mind, having compassion one of another, love as brethren, be pitiful, be courteous:* [9] *Not rendering evil for evil, or railing for railing: but contrariwise blessing; knowing that ye are thereunto called, that ye should*

*inherit a blessing.* [10] *For he that will love life, and see good days, let him refrain his tongue from evil, and his lips that they speak no guile:"* (**1 Pet. 3:8-10**)

Wisdom Calls Out To You

# CHAPTER 3

# THE KEYS OF THE KINGDOM: THE POWER OF PRAISE & PRAYER

## MY ENCOUNTER WITH THE ANGEL OF THE LORD

*"The LORD is my strength and song, and is become my salvation.* [15] *The voice of rejoicing and salvation is in the tabernacles of the righteous: the right hand of the LORD doeth valiantly.* [16] *The right hand of the LORD is exalted: the right hand of the LORD doeth valiantly."* **Psalms 118:14-16**

My wife and I with our kids faced a difficult situation. We struggled financially and looked for a place to live. It was a low point in our life. I sought for a way to explain to my four-year-old son why we were moving again. Even then, we made up our minds that we'd obey God's instruction and it was simple, to *PRAISE HIM even in the midst of a storm!* My tearful prayers and praise filled the night as I looked to heaven for an answer. I cried myself to sleep *still determined and still praising God though contrary to how I felt about the situation.* Praise made sense when there was something to praise for, but this wasn't the case. I was about to learn God's perspective, a new revelation about the power of praising God.

At about 2.30 am, a bright beaming light stood like a pillar next to me on my left side. I thought someone's turned the lights on. I opened my eyes to investigate and to my astonishment, the glory of Heaven stood in my room. I shook with awe when I heard a voice from the bright light saying to me,

*"I am the Angel of the LORD, the one spoken of in* **Psalms 34:7-8**

*"The angel of the LORD encampeth round about them that fear Him, and delivereth them.* [8] *O taste and see that the LORD is good: blessed is the man that trusteth in Him."*

*"God sent me to come to you this very hour because He heard your cries."* He moved aside to show me something, *"Look I've come with 12 Captains of the Legions of God's Angels."*

I remembered how Jesus spoke of the 12 legions of angels (**Matt. 26:53**). Twelve beaming lights stood in equally spaced ranks behind him. As I beheld the might of the Heavenly warriors before me, it was like a guard of honour, and the Angel of the Lord stood as the Heavenly Guard Commander. The towering warrior-angel then spoke in a firm voice,

*"I have come with a message to give to you. God sent me according to **Psalms 91**"* (which says),

> *"He that dwelleth in the secret place of the most High shall abide under the shadow of the Almighty. $^2$ I will say of the LORD, He is my refuge and my fortress: my God; in Him will I trust. $^3$ Surely He shall deliver thee from the snare of the fowler, and from the noisome pestilence. $^4$ He shall cover thee with His feathers, and under His wings shalt thou trust: His truth shall be thy shield and buckler. $^5$ Thou shalt not be afraid for the terror by night; nor for the arrow that flieth by day; $^6$ Nor for the pestilence that walketh in darkness; nor for the destruction that wasteth at noonday. $^7$ A thousand shall fall at thy side, and ten thousand at thy right hand; but it shall not come nigh thee. $^8$ Only with thine eyes shalt thou behold and see the reward of the wicked. $^9$ Because thou hast made the LORD, which is my refuge, even the most High, thy habitation; $^{10}$ There shall no evil befall thee, neither shall any plague come nigh thy dwelling.*
>
> $^{11}$ ***For He shall give His angels charge over thee, to keep thee in all thy ways.*** *$^{12}$ They shall bear thee up in their hands, lest thou dash thy foot against a stone. $^{13}$ Thou shalt tread upon the lion and adder: the young lion and the dragon shalt thou trample under feet. $^{14}$ Because he hath set his love upon me, therefore will I deliver him: I will set him on high, because he hath known my name. $^{15}$ He shall call upon me, and I will answer him: I will be with him in trouble; I will deliver him, and honour him. $^{16}$ With long life will I satisfy him, and shew him my salvation."*

As I stood utterly dazzled, the Angel of the LORD had a few more things to reveal, *"I also came with one more important angel who I want you to meet in person."*

As he finished saying these words, in a flash the vision changed and the Holy Spirit lifted me into the dining room where I found myself seated at the table. Soon after, I looked and saw a man garbed in business-like attire enter the room. He was about 6 feet 5 inches tall. He came in and sat at the other end of the table. It felt like a job interview and the boss had just walked in. He carried a different kind of authority not the same as that of the Angel of the LORD and the Twelve Captains. Theirs was the powerful and glorious might and force of God. His was a sense of splendour and richness that filled the air, in a different way. Dressed finely like a flamboyant businessperson, he wore a black, blue and silver striped, long-sleeved shirt, which ran vertically matching his pants, and he wore a leather belt, which had a golden buckle. His blonde hair glittered with golden brown strands running in between. His eyes were as blue as the sky with a glossy finish. As he sat down with a smile of assurance that seemed to calm my nerves, he proceeded to introduce himself,

*"I am the Finance Minister of Heaven"*. I wondered, does Heaven really have a finance minister? Unaware that he knew my thoughts, he replied,

*"Yes, that's me. I coordinate all the resources of Heaven that are sent to earth."*

I was just digesting the thought of a heavenly finance minister when the vision changed again and I saw a man standing in the open. He spoke ungodly, vile words. Cursed words flowed out of his mouth like a filthy river. A green mist and slime flowed from his inner being and defiled his body causing it to be filled with darkness, as black as black could be **(James. 3:6)**. The worst…This awful stench rose up to heaven before the Throne of God and it disgusted God greatly. Just to think God smelled this unclean fetor frightened me **(Rev. 18:5)**. Then I watched the Heavenly Father turn His back on the soul that cursed **(Isa.**

**59:1-4, 9-12)** and refused to hear his ungodly words. The reek of sinful words appalled the Holy God very much so that no one could help the foolish man, and neither did God respond. All the man got was discontentment and rejection.

> *"So that the LORD could no longer bear, because of the evil of your doings, [and] because of the abominations which ye have committed; therefore is your land a desolation, and an astonishment, and a curse, without an inhabitant, as at this day."* **(Jer. 44:22)**

This revelation was new to me and made me realise the stark reality that when God turns His back on you all hope disappears. Here, I understood the seriousness of cursing with the tongue; it is complete rejection from God. Surely, there is no condemnation for those who are in Christ Jesus **(Rom. 8:1)** but this man's words didn't represent Christ. How then could he qualify? I was sad for his soul seeing an answer from God was impossible. Nevertheless, the Angel of the LORD insisted I keep watching, as the vision wasn't yet complete. I saw the man came to his end and realised his folly. What could he do to make right with God? A few seconds had passed while he sobbed. Then all of a sudden, his face lit up, and he knew what he had to do. Immediately, he changed his words. He began with words of repentance seeking God's forgiveness. He then went into blessing mode and the sooner he did, so was the transformation that occurred in his being. His words became a bright light of blessing, praise and worship to God. Every time he spoke blessing, the light grew brighter until the darkness vanished from his body.

He glowed like the Angel of the LORD that stood beside me radiant as the midday sun. I also noticed, with every godly word he spoke, there was a white mist that produced a sweet aroma it made my heart joyous and filled me with peace. I saw this fragrance rise to Heaven to the glorious Throne of God. The beautiful fragrance captured God's Attention. He turned His Face, determined to search out where it was coming from. Hallelujah! When the Face of Glory (*CHRIST*) looks on you, favour immediately follows. God smiled with great delight upon that man (**Isa. 54:8**). Not only was he now clean and filled with the luminous of the Spirit, he won God's favour and blessing. His words had turned the King of Glory's attention on him.

*"For all those things hath Mine hand made, and all those things have been, saith the LORD: but to this man will I look, even to him that is poor and of a contrite spirit, and trembleth at My Word."* (**Isa. 66:2**)

The Angel of the LORD then declared, *"That's what happens with every word we speak. Your praises have gone before the LORD. Even in your struggle and pain, you chose to praise Him instead of cursing your offenders or your circumstances. So God has looked upon you and found favour with you."*

I thought about a verse in the Bible as he spoke these words to me, *"The righteous cry out and the LORD hears and delivers them out of all their troubles."* (**Psa. 34:17**). The angel then said to me, *"God has sent me to watch the progress in your life and to ensure His WORD will be fulfilled for your sake because He has promised and He will not fail His Word."* I thought of **Psalms 37:23**, which says,

*"The steps of a good man are ordered by the LORD and He delights in his ways."*

And verse 37 says,

*"Mark the perfect man and behold the upright. For the end of that man is PEACE!"*

The glorious encounter ended leaving me speechless with shivers of wonder running through my body. How God loved me, so much He sent the best of His Army, the *elite of the angels*, to visit me and deliver His Word. What honour God bestows upon us and what love so great, we cannot fathom the ends of it.

My heart still pondered on the things the angel showed me. A holy reverence filled me as I meditated on the revelation of praise, so fresh it burned within my soul. I now understood what God meant by the Words *righteous* and *upright* and that it was my words of *righteousness (blessing)* that caused God to respond **(Ps. 34:7-22)**. God saw *faith* in my words and He imputed righteousness unto me. I could see how it connected with what the Apostle Paul wrote, "That faith comes by hearing the *spoken* Word of God."

Like the man in the vision, when we declare God's Word, it cleanses and sanctifies us. I have also learnt from this and many other encounters with God, that when God Himself comes to us or through His holy angels, it's not only because we have found favour with him, but because of the *significance of the message He is delivering*. On this occasion, God saw it was too important to hand it to a man, He intervened and delivered the message Himself.

## IS YOUR HEART FIXED ON GOD?

When Christ is your focus your faith is pure because you see only Him and nothing but Him. The raging storm will cease to exist when you give your undivided attention to God. By doing this, you are telling God to take charge of the storm. For some, It's not an easy thing, to hand everything over to God especially when one feels the need to be in control of their circumstances, but when you begin to feel the pressure what then becomes your next course of action? Here's my suggestion, LET GO AND LET GOD! How does one let go and let God? They do this by simply declaring God's Word.

> *"I will cry unto God Most High; unto God that performeth all things for me...My heart is fixed, O God, my heart is fixed: I will sing and give praise.* $^8$ *Awake up, my glory; awake, psaltery and harp: I myself will awake early.* $^9$ *I will praise thee, O Lord, among the people: I will sing unto thee among the nations.* $^{10}$ *For thy mercy is great unto the heavens, and thy truth unto the clouds.* $^{11}$ *Be thou exalted, O God, above the heavens: let thy glory be above all the earth."* (**Psa. 57:2, 7-10**)

There is *GLORY* that lies in your tongue and rises from your inner man as you focus on God and as your heart remains fixed on Him, God becomes the strength of your heart and your portion forever (**Psa. 73:25-26**). True praise bubbles out of your spirit because you no longer see the darkness and the storm that surrounds you but you see the Christ and the light of His Glory shining stronger for you. Christ is mightier than any storm and bigger than any problem you face.

> *"And that which fell among thorns are they, which, when they have heard, go forth, and are* **choked with cares and riches and pleasures of this life (THE STORM)**, *and bring no fruit to perfection."* (**Luke 8:14**)

When you fix your heart on God, no storm will move you. Your *inner man* is calm and at rest in the LORD (**Psa. 46:10**). Like the faithful lion-heart of Stephen, filled with the Holy Ghost as he fixed his eyes on Heaven even in the face of death.

> *"But he (Stephen), being full of the Holy Ghost, looked up steadfastly into heaven, and saw the glory of God, and Jesus standing on the right hand of God,* $^{56}$ *And said, Behold, I see the heavens opened, and the Son of man standing on the right hand of God."* (**Acts 7:55-56**)

It's time to praise God! It's time to let the Glory of the Spirit within rise and overflow upon our lives. It's time to let go and let God! Though the storm rages around us Christ stands firm and calls us to come to Him in faith (**Matt. 14:25-33**) / (**Luke 8:4-21**). The WORD of GOD is a glory-seed sown into our Hearts by FAITH. Faith combined with the Word creates results that glorify God and bring us favour. Sometimes, even as believers in Christ, there comes some point in our lives when the Word of God doesn't make sense to us. Even our daily Bible reading and our worship can become plain and tasteless.

This leads to what we assume, is a dry season and soon we fall into depression and confusion.

But Christ is above any storm you face today. His Word is glory- seed; the seed of transformation, healing, breakthrough and prosperity. A season of harvest depends upon the seeds by which this harvest came, and the good news is *GOD'S WORD is all season*. So if your heart is constantly fixed on His Word then you will never face a dry season. Who dares stand against you if you continually abide under the Shadow of His wings (**Psa. 91:1**). If God is for you who can be against you? (**Rom. 8:31**)

God didn't say you won't face storms. However, God does promise that He will be with you through every trial you face. God also promises that you will bear much fruit if you abide in His Word. To rest in God's Word means to hear it, sing it, speak it and live in it. That is what it means to have your heart fixed on God. If you're facing a storm right now there's no better time to put this wisdom into action. What are you waiting for? It's time for you to let go and let God!

## THE POWER OF PREVAILING PRAYER

*"He saith unto them, But whom say ye that I am?* [16] *And Simon Peter answered and said, Thou art the Christ, the Son of the living God.* [17] *And Jesus answered and said unto him, Blessed art thou, Simon Barjona: for flesh and blood hath not revealed it unto thee, but my Father which is in heaven.* [18] *And I say also unto thee, That thou art Peter, and* **upon this rock I will build my church; and the gates of hell shall not prevail against it.** [19] **And I will give unto thee the keys of the kingdom of heaven: and whatsoever thou shalt bind on earth shall be bound in heaven: and whatsoever thou shalt loose on earth shall be loosed in heaven.***"* **(Matthew 16:15-19)**

*Prayer or speaking God's Word by faith* is the key to unlocking and understanding God's master plan for us. Prayer like praise is a powerful weapon and key of God.

The desire to walk in the Spirit and experience God only comes as you remain constantly in prayer at His feet (**Heb. 11:6**).

Prayer is the *Power of God's Words* in your mouth. It is conversing with God. Yes, I'm talking about *prevailing prayer*. God's Word is higher than ours and how much more blessings flow as a result (**Isa. 55:10-11**). The topic of prayer is also a subject of its own and could fill up a whole book. But to discover wisdom; we should always pray (*put God's word of promise on our mouths*) (**1 Thess. 5:17**).

There is deep revelation and truth about the power of prayer and I intend to reveal specific points on it to enrich your life.

**Romans 10:17** says, *"Faith comes by hearing and hearing by the Word of God."*

What Paul is saying here is that faith cannot show up until the Word shows up. Someone's going to have to speak the Word so that Faith can be released. **The substance and evidence of faith are revealed when the Word of God is spoken.** Paint this simple process in your mind: First, the *Word* is spoken; this results in faith arising to grab a hold of the spoken Word, and then when faith is added to the creative power of the Word this releases open doors. So as we enter through those open doors of God, we then discover the wonders of God behind those blessed doors. Imagine unlocking all the doors of Heaven and causing God to pour out a blessing upon you that there will not be enough room to contain it (**Mal. 3:10**). **Prayer unleashes the fullness of God to change our lives**. Jesus voiced this truth about prayer,

*"Let your will be done in Earth as it is in Heaven."* (**Matt. 6:10**)

We should with passion and intimacy, own those Words and use their truth to unlock our blessings. Let us look at some powerful truths about prayer:
- Prayer builds confidence and establishes a strong foundation of security, courage and diligence.
- Prayer combined with praise and worship creates an atmosphere for growth and brings healing and revival.
- Prayer imparts clear direction and protects your vision and your blessing.
- Prayer opens and enlarges your heart to receive your blessing.
- Prayer takes you to that place in God's Presence where He touches your faith to create and there He gives you the desires of your heart.
- Prayer draws and releases God's miraculous power into your life and causes the impossible to become possible with God's hand on you.
- Prayer embraces and drives vision.

- In prayer, we repent, reconcile and are humbled before God.
- Prayer also helps to accomplish every purpose that God has set for us.
- Prayer elevates us into God's presence and refines us to accomplish His Kingdom purposes.
- Prayer creates an atmosphere for us to grow in God and also discover our true identity in Him.
- Prayer delivers power from on high.
- Steadfast prayer brings God's favour and clothes us with authority and power to be victorious in all circumstances.
- Prayer imparts wisdom for every circumstance in life and fills you with joy. Prayer silences your critics and promotes you with many blessings. If you need motivation and inspiration pray till you get into that place in God's presence where motivation and inspiration flow constantly.
- Prayer guards your heart. A healthy prayer life produces a hunger for God's righteousness, holiness and power to be made manifest. Those who lack prayer don't have a hunger for God.
- Prayer is the doorway breakthrough. Your transformation or breakthrough will not come until you pray.

**Your faith can only be activated when you release the Word within you.** For God to come and move in your life, you must first create a place and a way for Him to do this and that is through your prayer. **Prayer combined with worship touches the power and mysteries of the Word and prepares the heart to encounter God. God becomes real to us and His Power flows for us when His Word becomes real on the inside of us. Heaven flows when prayer flows.**

To put it differently, the realities of Heaven are received when the reality of God's Word takes hold of us and saturates our hearts through fervent prayer.

You can only reach this place in your prayer when you first understand that **prayer is *fellowship* with God.** When you invest your time with God by conversing with Him, you are honouring God. See it this way, if you were friends with the richest man in the world he would treat you differently from those who just want his money. It is not about how many times or how long you have prayed but **how many times you were *intimate* in your prayer and worship with Jesus our Lord.** God wants a relationship with you. Will you let him come into your life today?

God's Words are God's Keys. God has given us the *Keys of the Kingdom and the Kingdom of God is within us by the indwelling of the Holy Spirit* (**Luke 17:21**). If we do not use those keys we cannot unlock the Kingdom. Prayer is using the keys of the Kingdom to unlock the doors for us. God is steadfast to deliver us and if we are steadfast with the Word of God, then God will raise a standard against the enemy and bring us victory to the Glory of God's name.

**You see, the Holy Spirit and the Word of God upon your mouth is the power combination that summons a Divine intervention from God. So prayer enlarges your boundaries and allows the Holy Spirit to work on your behalf.** The Holy Ghost and the Word put together in your mouth summon heaven to move and act on your behalf to make the impossible become possible and deliver the miracles of God into your life. What moves God is your heart of faith in alignment with His words. Hallelujah! When faith is stirred in your heart by prayer, this causes you to seek Him. Those who seek God with all their heart will find God because God wants us to find Him.

God looks upon the humble in heart and He responds to the

contrite in spirit. God created us for a *divine expression* and that is to worship God in Spirit and in Truth (**John 4:23-24**). There is no limit to you reaching the glories of God when you faithfully worship Him and place His Words in your mouth in fervent prayer.

The Spirit who knows the heart of God delivers to you correctly all that you need, even above and beyond all that you could ever think and ask (**Eph. 3:20**). As you pray in the Holy Ghost what is in the heart of God is poured out to you and is made manifest in the natural by the Power of the Holy Spirit within you. This is part of your right and inheritance in Christ Jesus.

You can influence the spirit realm by the power of *fervent* prayer that takes God's Word and activates it. Words are spiritual and have a direct impact on the realm of the supernatural. **What you speak you will receive.**

Therefore, what you pray for will be released unto you and if you are steadfast in showering the realm of the spirit with your words of faith this will subsequently overflow into the natural realm for you. Prayer gives access to the supernatural in God to change the natural realm. Prayer is tuning into God's glory channel. **Many don't realise that a glory connection with God is a love connection with God** and it is through this union that the Spirit moves to work on your behalf.

Pray at all times, in every occasion; in season and out of season, both day and night. Pray even when you don't feel like it. Pray, my beloveds in Christ, pray. It may be that tonight God might choose to come to you and speak to you. One Word from Heaven will bend any situation to respond to your needs. Seek the Lord with all your heart for He is worthy of all things and in Him is all worthiness. If God created all things with wisdom, then we should be praying to Him for the wisdom to handle all things. It is not that you can't handle your blessing but that you need wisdom to handle it. If you are a good steward in the little things then God will give you bigger things to handle. In addition to this, the beginning and foundation of good stewardship is thankfulness that flows from the heart.

So I urge you to pray my brothers, pray my sisters; pray as Jesus did. For Jesus moved heaven by the power of prayer to influence the earth. Jesus walked in faith in the Holy Ghost through His time spent in cherished conversation with the Father and when He walked on the earth sickness, demons, darkness and death could not stand against Him. They had to bow down and give way to Him because the One who loves Him and sent Him was with Him. Prayer should build an intimate relationship with God and from that deep relationship is God able to command His glory to flow to you and through you. Jesus has given us the keys of the Kingdom (*HIS WORDS*) to unlock all doors in the supernatural to affect the earth. Jesus explained the link between the spirit realm and the natural realm by these Words,

> *"What you bind on earth shall be bound in heaven, and what you loose on earth shall be loosed in heaven."* (**Matt. 16:16-19**)

Your relationship with God through prayer should move heaven to shake the earth. Now that you know this revelation, there's no stopping you from achieving the blessings God has intended for you if you are diligent and intimate in God. When the Love of God takes over, it takes over indeed. **When prayer touches the heart of God, it touches everything else around you** (**Matt. 18:18**).

## IT IS WRITTEN

**IT IS WRITTEN** is a powerful *declaration* that was used by our Lord Jesus in the greatest of His own trials and temptations. Should we use it? Yes. God wants us to speak His Word and to pray His Word. When every time we raise a prayer to heaven it is a sweet-smelling offering unto God and it fills His Holy Place. Every prayer never goes unnoticed when we place God's Word in it. God is ever watchful over His Word. When our desire for God overshadows everything in our life, God aligns us with His Word and His Power, to bless us.

**To discover God through His Word is to discover the source of power.** Sometimes questions like, *"What makes you believe there is a God to whom we can raise our prayers?"* The answer is simple; there is power in His Word. **If you do not believe in God then you will not know God and you will not be able to speak His Words of life.** Only those who have embraced His Word and have soaked themselves in it can testify to the power and glory of the Word.

Some say they have read the *BIBLE* from cover to cover. Yet it is not enough to gain head-knowledge if it doesn't do anything to your heart. Much of what is written is relevant to us today. I have grown to love the Bible (the Word of God) and its wisdom and teachings. Try not to fight it; regardless of how many times we try to twist its principles, the Word can never contradict itself because it is given to us by God, who is the Truth. The Word of God is not just a spiritual-based book but the Book of the Holy Spirit and from it springs forth life and inspiration.

All the positive things that today's motivational speakers are now coming up with are nothing short of what is already found in the Bible. It is important to have the Word of God in our lives, as what we choose to live by is the canopy that forms over us. For those in Christ, it is the Holy Spirit of God, and for those in the world, it is the powers of this world.

The Words, *"It Is Written"* are prophetic Words that no one can alter. When God says, *"It Is Written"* He means it is written and none can change what He has decreed. *It is written that the Word of God in our hearts <u>must</u> bear fruit* because God chose and ordained us to be fruitful (**John 15:16**). When Jesus was tempted by the devil in the wilderness, Jesus could have said anything to the devil; instead, He stood on the most powerful Word, *It Is Written*. Jesus wasn't just in defensive mode. No, he was really in attack mode. The Messiah released Heaven's greatest weapon to overcome the enemy by reminding him,

*"I (God) wrote this and you can't amend what I've said."*

The devil's agenda was to attack the identity of Christ and the authority of the Word. Jesus knew what satan wanted: he craved power over the Christ. Satan used the same trickery he played with Adam and Eve in the Garden of Eden. Nevertheless, Jesus wouldn't give in. He reprimanded satan by speaking the Word. What Jesus was really doing was declaring His Dominion and Lordship over satan. Likewise, when you speak the Word, like Jesus, you are also declaring God's dominion and Lordship over the enemy. Even the devil and his demons know God and they fear Him; they fear the name of Jesus. The devil knows the power of the Truth because the Truth can set us free. And one truth that the devil knows very well is that if his kingdom is divided it will fall apart.

This is wisdom that even the devil cannot deny, ironic but true. I must assume the devil must struggle a lot in this area because he hates wisdom. But see this truth for yourself in life today. When we are divided we fall and when we are united we stand strong. The Word of God keeps our hearts united in the Spirit and this oneness brings us life and peace.

The devil also knows that the Word of God in our mouth is our weapon to overcome him. So place God's Word on your mouth and in your heart. Ensure it never leaves you, as in it lies your blessing and the wisdom needed for everything in life. Know that when you hold fast to God's Word you are walking in God's Covenant (**Isa. 59:21**).

## YOUR MOTTO - YOUR STANDARD

*Wealth and success can follow after me, but I will still follow after my God. Set your motto and change your life.*

**Your motto becomes your *standard* and your *decree*.** It holds the key to your inspiration and the focus to your drive. For me, this was my experience about setting a motto and what it did to my life. My motto became my standard and my decree. I lived by it and its words encouraged me to pursue purpose with meaning. You can say *mottos* are wisdom quotes that stand out from the rest and move your heart. I had many mottos and I knew them all by heart because they became a part of my life and influenced the decisions I made. As a result of these wisdom quotes I had zeal for the prize laid before me and I was governed by what I believed in. Regardless of how down and low I felt, it was always that one Word of inspiration that came at the right moment to pick me up and guide me on. When I held fast to that word, courage held fast to my heart, determination drove me forward and God's strength caused me to soar.

**My motto became my mentor because from it I drew strength to persevere and conquer.** Even when I was struggling with a decision a fresh breath of wisdom would always come. Wisdom was always there to inspire me through the storm because I hung onto the standard that had kept me. What standard are you leaning on today? By words, is our world created, and by words, is our world destroyed. It can take only one Word from God to transform any life. It can take only a few words of wisdom to sit in your heart and bring out the best in you and that's what a motto can do. This book is filled with wisdom quotes and faith declarations. I encourage you to apply them in your life. Here's one of those mottos that influenced my life:

*"When you ask, believe and only believe and you will receive what you ask!"*

There is so much revelation you can dig out from this one motto. Have a resilient and warrior-like faith. Be hungry; be so hungry for your success that it will possess you and make you take the necessary steps needed to achieve that success. Although there is more in those few lines I will leave it to you to dig out the rest for yourself as the Spirit leads you.

For those who haven't yet done so, if you cultivate wisdom in this manner, soon you will reap the fruits of abundance that you want to see in your life.

Wisdom Calls Out To You

# CHAPTER 4

# THE VALUE OF THE POWER WITHIN —USE YOUR GIFT

*"For the heart that seeks God is the heart that will raise the standard by the Spirit within and win the crown of life from the LORD."*

A gift is from the heart. Yet that's not enough to tell you what it really is. So what is a gift? It's your time and service to others, your faith in God and when you give with the heart. A gift also can be that special ability, which defines who you are. You have a gift within. If you believe in Christ then the Power of God (the Holy Spirit) dwells within you to release God's abundance on you (**Eph. 3:21**). What you have within you is an important key that determines what you will have tomorrow. Let me explain. In **Matthew 25:14-30**, Jesus compared the Kingdom of Heaven to a man who gave talents (gifts or money) to his three servants expecting them to make good use of the gift and invest it to get more out of it. Two of the servants did just that and doubled the amount they invested, but the other failed to understand the intent of his master, instead, he went and buried it. To this servant Jesus called Him wicked and lazy with the advice given in the form of a question, why didn't you invest it so I could get interest from it? And Jesus concluded by saying,

*"For unto everyone that hath shall be given, and he shall have abundance: but from him that hath not shall be taken away even that which he hath."* (**Matt. 25:29**)

In other words, Jesus was saying to use what little you have because if you are faithful at the small things God will add more to it. You have something inside of you. Don't bury your gifts, use them. **Your worthiness is determined by how well you use your gifts.**

If you seek to bless the LORD with the small you have, the LORD will multiply it and cause you to inherit bigger things. It is about appreciating what little you have and investing it to receive an interest from it. **Power is only given and released where power is due.** Meaning, you have power within you to use but if you don't use it then it is worthless to you and others; only activated potential releases power. **Create a place for the LORD to fill and God will be faithful to fill it up. God is not asking you for what you don't have but only what you have.** Let me give you an example; I knew my calling was to preach the Gospel of peace, power and truth but I couldn't preach because I thought I had no one to preach to, to fulfil this calling. I was limited by what I thought. But I was wrong. God's Spirit spoke to me one day and told me to start preaching to nature; yes, the trees, the stones, the air, literally everything that surrounded me.

So I began preaching to the four walls of my room every time when the Spirit of the LORD came upon me, I would just let it loose and flow with it. Immediately when I activated this gift and ministry to preach God's word, I felt there was a crack in me that eventually became large enough for a gush of blessing to overflow into my life. My gift was now useful because *I did something with it.* God began to open the doors for me to preach the Word on pulpits and fellowship meetings almost immediately as soon as I began to release the gift from within and was steadfast at it. God's not waiting for you to be perfect so He can use you. Rather, God is looking for your *willingness*.

**Your gift is your seed. Plant it and you will reap a great harvest from it.** Your seed has the potential to become a tree that will bear more fruits and those fruits themselves contain seeds that if planted will become more trees which will bear more fruits. **Your words are also seeds. Your service is a seed and your giving is a seed. If one seed has the potential to become a plantation then we should plant more seeds so that we can harvest plantations.**

If the word or gift within you has the intent and potential to help someone else then it shouldn't be kept hidden but revealed to the world. It is not about how many people will like it, it is about who gets helped by it. Even if it's only one person out of a hundred then you have achieved something, because you used your gift to help someone.

Your obedience to God's voice in releasing your gift to benefit someone else could mean you not only helped them, but may have also saved their life. It could be something as simple as a *smile* or *a kind word*.

I can't remember where I read this story, but there was a man who was at the end of his life and thought there was no longer any hope for him. He was ready to end it all and commit suicide. He woke up that morning and planned to go find the tallest building and throw himself off it. But there was still a glimmer of hope in him, like one last desperate attempt to see the light of life. He cried out to God and then said to himself, *"If, on my way to kill myself, only if I pass at least one person who smiles or says a kind word to me, then I won't take my life and I will erase the thought of it from me altogether."* Imagine, now if you were one of those individuals whom he passed by that very morning.

**Surely, you smile to receive a smile, a gift given means more given back to the giver,** and how wonderful is the truth, when the gift you give saves someone else's life? If disappointment or discouragement shows up in the middle of your attempts to do something good, don't stop, release that gift anyway. It's not about the critics, it is about the beneficiary. Even Jesus had to put up with the critics but that wasn't going to stop Him from doing the Father's Will. He was going to save the world anyway.

Even for me, if this book helps just ten people out of a thousand then I still have achieved something. You play your part and plant the seed, and God will pour the rain and sunshine to make it grow. **Any gift used has power. It only depends on if you use it and how much you use it.**

**Your greatest challenge firstly is you.** The intentions of your heart set your purpose; for they will always reveal what drives you from within. **Glory is not yet glory until you find it in the place that belongs to you.** God appoints to each one of us the blessings we deserve according to the purposes in our hearts.

Only there and then are you truly complete when you find that place ordained by the LORD for you. **We can plant a seed but**

**it takes the Word and Spirit of God to give it sunlight and water for it to grow**. If the seed is not planted it will not sprout and grow. Act now without hesitation or compromise and know that you are doing the right thing before the eyes of God. **It is the fact to the *fact* and the truth to the *truth* that we blossom in Christ and apart from Christ we can do nothing.** Let Christ take the gift within you and make it flourish.

# THE GENEROUS HEART IN CHRIST

When we speak of the standard within, at what level can we place a generous heart? I'll tell you; at the highest level. Being generous is not really, because you have plenty to give. Rather, it is when we have given with the heart. The generous heart is warm. A cold heart is like the frost of the night. But **a warm heart is like the rising sun in winter's cold.** Seasons will come and go, but the reward of the faithful and righteous will always remain and their fruit will be luscious both in season and out of season. **The heart of the generous man sees the blessing of tomorrow and cultivates the hearts of others to prosper and find peace.**

**The heart of the generous seeks to bless, and in doing so will receive a hundredfold blessing in return.** I don't know about you but if I am reaping a hundred-fold, that's a high level of yield. Indeed generosity opens the floodgates of Heaven. However, the main player in this is not in the outward action, to display oneself proudly. **True generosity is of the HEART.** Give with the heart for it has a powerful effect and influence. The heart's greatest reward is when you give without holding back when you love because it means everything, when you find peace and rest from your struggles, and when you trust because trust is the backbone of any nation and people.

**The heart is worth more than the riches of this world, it is the richness of this world.** Out of the heart flows the issues of life (**Prov. 4:23**). The standards you set in life are standards from your heart. God looks at the heart of man and not his outward appearance (**1 Sam. 16:7**). If we have the mind of Christ (**1 Cor. 2:16**) then we should also have the heart of Christ. The sky is no longer the limit because of the infinite Christ in us. You can achieve greater things than what you've already attained and grow beyond what your mind can conceive because of Christ in you.

**The supernatural should be natural to us. When we look beyond our impossibilities we perceive the possible in God.** When we realise we can reach limits beyond our human capacity, the supernatural becomes real to us. The supernatural is meant to be normal because our God owns the supernatural. The supernatural is our inheritance and so the natural should take on the nature of the supernatural. What am I getting at? There can be no higher standard than God Himself and His ordination upon us. **When the glory of Christ rises upon us He increases the standard in our hearts and our potential for greater things** (**Eph. 1:18-19**). Our hearts were created to reach their full potential. We are called to bless others and this is the ultimate place given to man. God's calling 'to bless' supersedes every other calling.

**Our calling has come from the highest office with the approval of the highest authority; God.** To bless is a righteous thing. God has never forsaken the righteous but only promoted them and increased their blessings. No one can change what God ordains. So if the commission and call to bless is for every man, then we are sure to receive an overflow of abundance from God. This is an ultimate command even the angels cannot bend because God has sworn by His own name to bless the generous- heart.

So seek God with your heart and He will show you the way to go. It's about experiencing God's abundance within to express it on the outside. **When the heart believes then the heart will perceive. Every time you believe, you sow seeds of faith in God. That releases the Kingdom's riches.**

**So let God lead your heart and you will not have to worry about how to get there.**

## THE 'STANDARD' OF YOUR WORDS

Watch your words and actions because they flow from the heart. The standard you set in life is determined by what you encourage in your life. To bless and live in Christ is the highest standard but to walk after the lusts of this world is lowering your standards to the level of the flesh. **By your own words and actions shall you raise the standard or you can easily give it away to your fleshly desires.**

It is you who decides the outcome of your blessing. Like I mentioned earlier every word we speak is the fruit of our mouth and reveals the standard in our hearts. The *true*, the *noble* and the *faithful* are those who know that with every word spoken is power to create either good or evil. The measure that you set for others is the same measure that will be measured back to you (**Luke 6:38**). When words are taken lightly then destruction and failure loom at the doorstep. **No one likes to hang around a loose-mouthed person because all he produces is bitter water. Your words reveal your standard.** Every idle word spoken means a shallow heart that is grounded in greed, pride, lust, and foolishness. Kind words, however, are a fountain of life.

The reverence and wisdom of God is to keep your tongue from speaking evil and to uphold the Testimony of Jesus Christ. Just as the light of the sun brightens up the day so must the Word of God in your heart. Heaven recognises the little things you do for others. So **speak only what God has ordained as a mouth full of generosity reveals a heart full of blessing.**

## BLESS YOUR CHILDREN

If you are a parent, your kids need you to be more than just a parent. They need you to be their mentor and an example of good living and success as whether you realise it or not, you are their greatest influence. Their little hearts hang onto your progress because what you choose in life will also affect them. Your discipline, your love, your leadership and your guidance are everything they need for a successful and abundant life. Thus, you are not only their mother or father, you are not only their caretaker, but you are also their standard and their inspiration.

Teach them in the way of life and wisdom and they will never depart from it. Build in them a prosperous and free-spirited attitude so that they may pursue purpose with diligence. Trust in God's wisdom and don't ever doubt your own abilities. God gave them to you for a reason. That reason defines who you are and that's why you are here. Always keep your head up high and move forward for the sake of your children's progress. Believe only in God and He will provide the way for growth.

Remember, the little you have is enough for God to make something out of. The most important thing of all for your child's future is how you build them in Christ. You must *BLESS*

*THEM* if you want to see them succeed in life. I intentionally wrote those words in capital letters to make my point. **A father and a mother's blessing will launch their children's lives into great success, prosperity and abundance.** So you play a very important role as the one whose words of blessing will carry their child into great heights of success. Now, if you have been calling your child, "You good for nothing!" You need to immediately, change that (repent of it) and say,

> *"You are perfect for every good thing in God. In fact, you are highly favoured by the LORD. I love you, my child. I am proud of you. And you can expect to achieve anything great in life and prosper in everything you do because you are the best for your purpose. I bless you with the blessing of God and let that blessing remain on you forever."*

You can add more words to it, but I've given you something to start with. Do this act of blessing as often as you can. Speak into your children's lives and you will see *blessings* will never leave your house but flourish in every way, shape and form. Don't waste a moment to bless your child. Pause right now, and call your son and daughter over to you (if they are nearby). Lay your hands on them and speak your words of blessing over their lives.

Do you know why children are rebellious? It's because we keep cursing them. As Godly parents, it's not because you are disciplining them the wrong way, almost any parent knows discipline is important in raising your child the right way, but they rebel because of the way they are spoken to. **When discipline turns into irritation and constant annoyance to insanity, then bitterness sets in, and the crippling curse destroys, all that is left are broken pieces and ruined lives (Eph. 6:4).** What begins as a loving home can deteriorate into hate. When revulsion consumes a child, pride enters and the result is disappointment and destruction. I once met a young man in his twenties who'd just come out of drugs. In his clear mind, he said to me, *"All I ever wanted was to hear my mum say, 'I love you son.' But all she told me was how worthless I am, and I believed it."*

He cried so bitterly over this as he revealed his hurt masked by years of violence and drug abuse.

Many times when we discipline our children anger gets the better of us and we begin cursing them. Those heavy words will remain on their innocent hearts and minds and sadly they will never flourish until someone else lifts or breaks the curse with words of blessing. And, what better person to do this than the parent of the child? *Please! Please! Please!* If this wasn't true and so important, I wouldn't have bothered about it, but it is. If there is one important thing you can take away from this book it's this. **Bless your children and you will see the positive growth in their lives.** If you're a mentor, teacher, coach, guardian, or leader, this same truth also applies to you.

## THE POWER OF GOD'S PEACE

*"Thou wilt keep him in perfect peace, whose mind is stayed on Thee: because he trusteth in Thee."* **(Isaiah 26:3)**

When you find that place of peace with God, why ignore it? Peace is obviously better than worry and stress. **You hear God better in the place of peace and receive clear direction from Him when your heart is at rest.** God wants you to find rest and inspiration in Him. He wants you to be still and know He is God; to discover His love and peace for your soul and your future. **When peace floods your soul and overtakes you it will always point you to your solution and lead you to your breakthrough.**

Peace brings oneness of the heart and so it also brings favour and anoints the heart with courage and strength. **The purposes of the heart are established when the heart is in a place of peace**. When you find your place of peace then you find your song and rhythm for life.

**To believe in you and all that you are is a gift of life and one to treasure. To believe in the goodness of life in God is the patrician call of wisdom.** To bless is the noble cause of man, a piece of heaven revealed through us on earth, so the more we bless the more of heaven we have with us.

**The same God who commanded us to go and be fruitful also commands His peace to be poured upon us through Jesus Christ.** This eternal peace is untouched by the unclean, dark forces of this world and is bounded by the eternal Covenant of Peace that God made with us (**Ezek. 37:26**).

**The peacemaker belongs to God and his fruit is precious before the Most High.** Imagine a world without peace. That's undoubtedly World War III, and will probably be the most horrific war ever in man's history. However, we who are in Christ have peace. If peace abides in your heart, with it is a sweet fragrance of God's righteousness (**Jas. 3:18**). Where there is no peace there is nothing but vanity, bitterness, hate, destruction and darkness. Go too deep and you'll fall into this deep pit of darkness and never be able to come out on your own.

God can deliver the oppressed and save the lost soul. All you have to do is reach out to Him and call on His Name and He will save you. Reach high enough to Heaven where God sits in His entire Splendour and Glory. You are meant to walk in goodness but **without the peace of God how can you experience the fullness of God? True prosperity means 'heart-peace' and this**

**releases God-knowledge. When the knowledge of God burns in the heart of man like fire, he will go forth and be a light to the world.**

The proud think they have nothing to fear, they enforce corruption to remove the peacefulness of man by their arrogance. This is utter foolishness. Those who think their corrupt wealth is proof of their wisdom will soon find out that wickedness will chase after them.

**Wealth acquired in an ungodly way will bring destruction, grief and a curse to the one who bears this wealth.** Wealth acquired dishonestly vanishes instantly like smoke in the wind, never to be seen again. Do not be conceited in your ways for the paths of wickedness lead to hell and its ending is destruction.

The sinful and evil thoughts of the wicked man are supported by the devils and his heart is far from the light. Until the light comes to him he knows no good thing but to steal, kill and destroy like his father the devil (**John 8:44**) / (**John 10:10**). But seek peace with all man and with God for this is a noble cause and one that will teach you true humility and bring you many rewards.

## FAITH IS ALL YOU NEED

*Your FAITH in God's Word gives God a reason to ACT.*

The most gracious and sincere thing mankind can ever do for themselves is to embrace faith in God and His Word. The walk of faith cannot be described in one paragraph. For with faith is hope and both are founded on love. **And nothing speaks greater faith than the name of Jesus.** He who does not believe in Christ curses his own soul to death. Faith works by love through Christ (**Gal.**

5:6).

Trust the Lord's safe hands. He will hold you up at all times. God never turns a blind eye to your silent prayers. Choose the majestic and honourable things in life, like humility and faith, and you choose a good thing because God rewards humility and faith. The power to achieve your dream is always at the edge of your fingertips. It all depends on your faith, your confession and a matter of time. Don't give up too soon as the good things in your life are too precious to give up on. God has a plan for you and it is a plan to prosper you in every way. Brethren, be courageous, be faithful and be strong in the LORD.

**If faith pleases God then the man of faith is but the most powerful tool of difference that any nation needs.** He is a tool in God's Hand to shake kingdoms and move mountains. And you and I are exactly that. When we were created, faith was also implanted in our spirit and soul thus faith is an innate part of us. We activate faith by what we declare, so I say boldly to you,

*"The LORD bless thee, and keep thee:* [25] *The LORD make His face shine upon thee, and be gracious unto thee:* [26] *The LORD lift up His countenance upon thee, and give thee peace."* (**Num. 6:24-26**)

For God to complete His work in you and I He must unite our hearts first. **True faith is the oneness of the heart. Peace thrives where unity exists.** The Force of Faith achieves a mighty blow on the enemy when it is fixed on God. **So let your heart be united in faith and you will find the peace to prosper and the power to overcome.** The oneness and pureness of faith is the strength of the heart. The pureness of believing brings the reward of God, for the believing heart pleases the Lord. With wisdom is found many treasures, and **those who purchase wisdom with the diligence-**

**of-faith, have invested in the favour of *our LORD*.**

Walk in humility and faith in God and you will never be disappointed. Give ears to wisdom and you will walk in Divine favour. Faith touches the power and substance of the Word and is the holy evidence of the power of God in our lives. With faith comes purpose and diligence. Let me explain. There are things that the LORD wants you to have and perhaps achieve along the way toward your ultimate purpose in life. These *Divine Favours* will eventually come to you without fail to be fulfilled in your life if and only if, you are faithful to stay on the path of diligence to His Word by your faith. **The manifestations of faith become strong when we are *fervent in prayer*.** Those who walk by faith walk in the Spirit and the Word. **Where true faith is, the spirit of man rejoices and experiences freedom.**

You either believe in the right things or the wrong things. When you feel miserable it's because you are doing something miserable. Get out of it and give your mind a break. You must find your place of inspiration. By this, I mean a *physical place* like a nature park, a beach view or a quiet place to get your mind off the problem and onto the solution.

**INSPIRATION is like a TRAIL to the TREASURE BOX. Wherever the trail of inspiration begins, FOLLOW IT.** Furthermore, **the starting point of CHANGE is to ACCEPT CHANGE no matter how you may feel about it, even in distress and misery.** Don't settle with wretchedness. Become your solution and just get up and go forth towards your breakthrough and victory. Worry stresses the heart and achieves nothing, but faith eases the heart and produces strength to overcome. Faith perceives the outcome and goes after it.

Ask yourself this question, would you be happy if you

achieved that desire in your life? All it takes is your faith. Faith aligns with the will of God and draws the resources of Heaven to fulfil your assigned purpose on earth.

Be associated with those who have mountain-moving faith and you will see that they simply obey God's Word and follow it. **You find your voice and identity in what you believe in and this shapes your character and your life**. To possess your true identity you must believe in who you are and what you want to be in life. If you are purpose and mission-oriented you will have a clear-cut good influence on others. **Faith does not only perceive the result but faith is the motivation and direction that will get you to the result**.

We know that faith without action is dead. The question is what is the "action?" It is obedience to God's Word. So **faith without obedience to God's Word is dead.** The results you get in life are dependent on the actions you take for these results and the determination you enforce behind those actions.

# VALUE

When you have learned the fruit of faith you have also learned the value of faith meaning what you believe in is what you value. If your characteristics are consistent with your values, then your character is valuable to this generation. Why are values so important? It is because they protect and embrace life. If you value life, then you are most likely one that makes life work for you. **The more valuable someone or something is the greater their potential for success; because success is equal to the value we put behind it.** Therefore, always strive to add value to your life and the lives of others. That also is another true secret of success; by this, I mean how much value you put into others is the worth they produce. The greatest value you can give to anyone is the Gospel of Jesus Christ and His Salvation.

Pride always puts a dent in the value of anything you build that is why it is so important to guard your heart against pride. If you think you know how to get there, don't forget to take good advice from others on your way there, and don't let arrogance swallow you up. If you are too stubborn and reluctant about learning wisdom your pride will eventually steal your joy and success away from you.

**Success itself is not a happening it is a decision we make. Have you decided to succeed? Have you chosen to change?** You are the main effort that gives reason to everything that crosses your path in life, and if you choose the good, you will have the good.

# FAITH FOR A RIPE HARVEST IN GOD

We are only limited by what we believe. If you want life, then choose life, but don't stay in the middle. Faith cannot work where confusion and doubt exist; they are enemies.

> *"Knowing this, that the trying of your faith worketh patience. [4] But let patience have her perfect work, that ye may be perfect and entire, wanting nothing. [5] If any of you lack wisdom, let him ask of God, that giveth to all men liberally, and upbraideth not; and it shall be given him. [6] But let him ask in faith, nothing wavering. For he that wavereth is like a wave of the sea driven with the wind and tossed. [7] For let not that man think that he shall receive anything of the Lord. [8] A double-minded man is unstable in all his ways."* **(James 1:3-8)**

By faith, you can harvest the fruits of wisdom and the rewards of life. The pursuit of the heart is with faith. **Inward belief and confidence coupled with vision, is an ingredient for powerful experiences in life**. More so, the pursuit of excellence is not an overnight thing, but it is achievable by the power of vision and diligence for destiny that lies in our hearts, planted in us by God. This is what the Holy Spirit uses to direct you in the way you should go. If you are yet unable to see the wisdom in these words then you have completely missed the knowledge that comes with it. **Seek to understand the wisdom and the power of God within you then you will have knowledge to prosper**.

If you don't take the first step on the path of righteousness right now, then how do you expect to see the good end that you desire? It is not that God's forgotten you but that you've lost your way. Turn your heart back to the way of righteousness and you will reap the fruits of your desired outcome.

All you've got to do is to have faith, take a bold step and walk the righteous path without hesitation. Don't wait for someone else to tell you. You can make that decision right now and begin your journey to success. Get up and go my friend, get up and go! Persevere with patience because limitations come when we are not patient. **Don't settle for second best because God wants to give you the best. Don't settle for good enough because God can provide more than you ask or think. Impatience, is like an unripe fruit which is sour and inedible; if we harvest it too early we only taste the bitter immaturity of it.**

**Immature or raw potential cannot reap full-grown success unless it is first groomed.** You must be both patient and diligent when building your potential to reap a ripe harvest. Many times we fall not only because of our immaturity but because we are not consistent with our faith to cultivate abundance. Hence, Faith with patience will produce the consistency required to reap a full harvest.

**The true test of passion and determination includes patience and perseverance.** Passion without patience is like a candle blown out in the wind before its time. While determination without vision is like clouds without rain or like the sun without light and heat needed to warm and brighten the earth. **To be truly successful, you must embrace the truth that what you start you must finish.** Hang in there long enough and you will be the master of your own life, under the wisdom and direction of God. Some things are worth waiting for. Wait patiently for what you desire, for when it is ready, it will come to you as a complete package. **Give your heart for your cause as that is what makes you who you are.** Remain firm for your blessing. Wait for it diligently until it comes to you fully in its beauty and perfection. Patience results in positioning. Hence, **be persistent and your diligence will make you a pillar in the house of the wise.**

## CHOOSE PEACE OR ANGER

Many sick things in life are a result of sin. Anger that leads to sin and corruption is one of them. It is sickness to the soul and on a larger scale, the devastation of humanity. You are certainly not going to achieve anything by being angry at God and the good things in life. Anger doesn't achieve any righteous purpose, but only serves to bind the heart with bitterness. **Anger creates limitation in the heart, but peace provides us clear understanding to extend our boundaries.**

From the cradle of peace, our hearts find truth that can set us free from the clutches of darkness, foolishness, prejudice, hate, bitterness, unforgiveness, and pride. **If you're always angry at others you'll end up having no friends to comfort you in your**

**time of need.** If you choose anger you are like bitter water that no one wants to drink and it will end up being poured out. If you are always frustrated and stressed you too will also have no friends to stand with you. They'll eventually steer away from you because they can't handle your excessive derangement. So then why would you choose a miserable life filled with anger when you can choose the freedom of God?

Today God is still reaching out to help you whether you realise it or not. He wants to give you wisdom to direct your path. The peace of God reveals to us true humility that liberates us and causes us to see the light of wisdom. **If you want to pursue the truth in any matter, pursue peace first and then you will find Truth.**

**Because Christ is not only *Truth* He is also *Peace*.** If you want to be free from a life of dryness and emptiness, start with peace and God will lead you into all truths by His Spirit.

Many will argue that God doesn't answer prayers. The truth is that, what you don't believe in, you won't receive because the heart applies the substance of faith. If you don't believe in God then how can you receive from God? You will never know what the apple tastes like until you bite into that apple yourself. If you have not encountered God in a deep way or His peace for that matter then how can you (not yet reaching a place of understanding) pass judgment on others who endeavour to find God? **Anger is not a good judge, but those who walk in peace possess insight and understanding to judge righteously.** God wants us to walk in peace so that we can discover and experience the mysteries of His glory. The way of peace is pleasant to those who find it.

## RESILIENT HOPE AND LOVE

*Hope looks at the face of the storm and tells It, your time is up. Because with Hope is Love and Love perseveres.*

When the storm comes to disappoint you try the power of hope. Circumstances can challenge you to your breaking point and knock you down, but if you have hope, you have healing, strength and the *power of praise* on your lips. **Walk in the hope of the Spirit and your joy will never depart from you.** With hope is also favour and honour. **Hope is closeness with God for it is the resilience of God, aggressive against the darkness and victorious over any adversary.** With hope is *praise*.

If you've been cursed and criticised up to this point, know that if you have hope, you're untouchable. If you keep up with *hope* it will bring you through any circumstance and into the sunlight of your success. It is this hope that makes a difference in your life.

**Hope is resilient because it is woven with faith and love.** God's true call to worship is for His children to walk in faith, hope and love.

So let's talk a little bit more about love. True sacrifice is with love. Love makes a way where there is no way because God's love can see through the storm when all else fails. **The pathway of love in your heart is also reflected in the respect you give to others.** Embrace the good in others and God will bless you with great peace. Reach out to others in love and the lesson of love will never depart from them. They in return will always cherish your lovingkindness and gentle hand. For with love, there is a perfect way. I would rather give love than have nothing with it.

I would rather tell those close to my heart that I love and care for them because life is too short to hold a grudge. **When parents show love to their children it is a gift from the heart.** Love then becomes the guiding light for us to follow and the manual from which to raise our children in the best way granted by God. Show your children the right way to go and they will always treasure and cherish the love you have shown them. In return, they will be good to you in your old age and bring you honour when your hair is grey. But a child who denies the love of his parents brings grief to their heart. **The child does not realise that love is a gift that will build his character and sharpen him for success.** If you have been running from your parents or have not yet made peace with them, today is your day to do so. I urge you to return to them; call them up and see how they are going and return to that gift of love that will bring you goodness in life.

**For with the love of God comes great favour and many blessings. Embrace the good in others and it will teach you how to love.** For love is the greatest commandment of the Kingdom of Heaven. Love governs every principle of the Kingdom of God. With love is wisdom. Those who walk in love will abide under the shadow of God's mighty wings. Don't take love for granted because it is the verified air of Heaven. The *righteous* know this truth that every great achievement in God is founded on the purpose of love.

# HONOUR

*"Honour and majesty are before Him (THE LORD GOD): strength and beauty are in His sanctuary (HOLY PLACE)."* **(Psalms 96:6)**

If we were to sum up God's will for us in one word it would be *Honour.* The underlying message of the Bible from Genesis to

Revelation is all about Honour—to God and man. The greatest commandment of God is love. **To love is to honour. Every form of sin is a violation of honour.** With honour is loyalty, and trust.

The principle of honour is this—**honour given horizontally, attracts honour that comes down from Heaven vertically.** What do I mean by this? **The governing essence of God's love is honour.** When you demonstrate the Love of God, you manifest honour. **When you possess *truth*, you possess *honour*.** God does all things in honour of His Covenant and Identity. **Honour is the crown of humility and the revelation of sincerity.** To have faith in God is to honour God. To accept His love is to accept His honour. With honour is the reverence of God.

**Psalms 96:6** has so much revelation in it about God and the word, *"honour."* With honour is *majesty* and both are set before the King of Glory, the LORD God of all creation. Both honour and majesty are surrounded by *strength* and *beauty*. What strength and beauty? The strength and beauty of God's glory, power and might. So if you want true honour, seek God's face first in humility and He will add with it, His majesty, strength and beauty.

If you ever want to be successful in life humble yourself and everything else that you desire will follow. Humility comes before honour, and pride before a great fall (**Prov. 15:33/ Prov.16:18**). A humble heart is like a jar made to hold the precious ointment of honour. It is like a basket woven to carry the delicious food made ready to bless others with. Those who seek after God with their hearts wear the heavenly coat of honour. **Possess humility and you will also be given honour and favour. God will always honour the heart that honours Him.** Embrace honour and it will embrace you. **Honour God with your best** and He will honour you with His *best—majesty, strength and beauty*. That's saying **'Mathew 6:33'** but in a different way. With honour is peace.

Remember, only thirty seconds of peace is worth more than a lifetime of vanity. **For those who follow peace with their heart will always find it in honour**. Honour is God's identity. When we received Jesus as our Lord and Saviour we also received His honour, majesty and strength. We became God's and He became ours. To demonstrate honour is to demonstrate the Kingdom of Heaven. *Honour reveals the character and attitude of God*. With honour is love, joy, peace, patience, kindness, goodness, faithfulness, humility and self-control. When honour is given and received it attracts the Presence of God. Therefore, *when honour is lacking in the House of God, so also will be the Power of God's Presence*.

## THE GREATEST IN THE KINGDOM

*"But ye shall not be so: but he that is greatest among you, let him be as the younger; and he that is chief, as he that doth serve."*
**(Luke 22:26)**

He that is the greatest amongst you is the one who serves. If you cannot handle small matters with a heart of service how can you handle the big ones? If the small matters are already too much for you, then the big matters will surely drown you and kill you. So having the heart of the servant is important because **a true leader cannot be effective until he has first learned how to serve others.**

**Only a man of true heavenly honour will wash the feet of another in humility.** Do for others what you would want them to do for you. If you bless them with a prophetic blessing you will receive a prophetic blessing. If you bless them with goodness you will receive goodness in return. If you bless with truth and loyalty you will receive both truth and loyalty. **The call of servanthood is not only to individuals but also to nations (Exod. 19:5-6)**. The poorest of nations is said to be the most troublesome of nations. But a nation that serves the Lord will prosper because the Most High God will make their wells overflow.

You must grasp that **your potential and capacity to increase is measured by the humility of your heart and by your attitude of service**. When you serve loyally, not to please man but to please God then you are sure to gain special favour and promotion. The goodness of your heart will first give you a good name and reap for you the rewards of life. When you learn to serve in your heart first then you will discover that there is no lack for those who open their hearts to serve.

The heart is like a river; block its path and you stop its flow. But let it run through and the flow will never stop for you. What this means is, that as long as you keep blessing and being a blessing the flow of blessing itself will continue in your life. **Out of the abundance of the heart, your true worth is revealed**. Do not confuse service with slavery. To serve with your heart is true service and this brings honour.

There is certainly no lack, for those who follow the footsteps of Christ, which is the footsteps of a faithful and humble heart. Christ only set out to do His Father's Will and to accomplish it even though He would lay His life down for us. *'His mission to serve His Father'* was His food, His water, His warmth and His comfort. Christ served because He wanted to. We then should also have the same attitude if we are in Him and are led by the Holy Spirit. We serve because we want to and not because we are forced to. Christ our Good Shepherd has left us an example to serve with our hearts. He is the Shepherd that leads our souls to quiet waters and makes us lie down in green pastures. He will keep us on the path of righteousness (**Psa. 23**).

If you want to partake in Christ, who is the Glory of God, then have a heart to serve like He did. *Every time you serve, you sow a seed of favour and blessing which is deposited into God's Bank.*

What you give to God, He multiplies and makes it overflow just like the two fish and five loaves. What little do you have? I urge you to invest it into God and He will multiply it for you (**Matt. 6:33**). It is a two-way process; serve first and you will be served (**Prov. 11:25**).

**Every man's prosperity or reputation lies in the truth about what service he provides that meets the needs of others**. A business service is a good example of service in action that reaps good results and a good reputation. The truth that lies in this is obvious; the better the service quality, the higher the reputation, and the greater the income and profit gained. I'm not implying you work till you collapse and die of exhaustion. What I'm saying here is that *when your service is required your service is treasured*. The value and worth of your service to God as His vessel becomes clear by the demand placed on it. Give what you have.

**Your ability to extend your influence is found in your ability to extend your heart to serve where the need is**. If you cannot serve in humility then you sacrifice quality for convenience. One other important thing I learnt about why we must serve is this; **you serve in humility to protect the gift, the anointing and the blessing that rests upon you. If you serve others wholeheartedly you will always be trusted with great things** In saying this, there is a definite link between *trust, favour* and *service*. So the serving heart will reap more rewards than the heart that refuses to help the needy.

Your heart of service may not only do good to someone else but could save a life. Save one life and you save thousands more. So how do you gain the favour of God? Easy! Serve God with all your heart, mind, soul and strength and God will concern Himself with you. He will perfect that which concerns you (**Psa. 138:8**). **Psalms 37:4** summarises this beautifully;

*"Delight yourself in the LORD and He shall give you the desires of your heart".*

I talk about purpose also in other Chapters of this book but there is a point to make concerning the serving heart. The man of purpose is recognised by what he pursues. He is a man with meaning in his life. To him, the world only exists to fulfil the purpose set for him which leads me to the point I want to bring across to you. **The true man of purpose was born to serve others and show kindness to them. This is the code of blessing for humanity. For those who serve others with their heart shall themselves be served.**

The man of purpose is not just like anybody. He is a great leader because he has a vision to serve powerfully. Anybody can have a vision but the vision of God can only be embraced in humility. Vision requires commitment and loyalty; the traits of "servanthood." **Our calling in life is eventually discovered when we have a heart to serve. So to find your calling in life, you must first learn to serve with your whole heart.**

We can sum it up in these Words, "where a man's heart is, is where his treasures lie" (**Matt. 6:21**). **Those who serve others are most likely the ones who eventually find their purpose and** calling in life.

The three words, "SERVICE—CALLING—FAVOUR" are all linked to each other. Do you want favour? Then serve with your heart. Do you want to find out what your calling is in life? Then serve with your heart, first to the LORD, and then to others. We all have a unique path to follow and if we pursue our goals with humility then our purpose is not far from us. **Great teachers and leaders are known for their heart of humility and their attitude when serving others.**

If you are a teacher embrace the good in your students and encourage them to soar out of their weaknesses and they will never forget you. If when they meet you again then they will show you great kindness and appreciation. They will shower you with many gifts. **They that sow in humility will reap an abundance of blessings from the LORD. They that sow in tears will reap in joy.**

**A day spent blessing and serving is better than a day filled with negativity. A day spent on worthy and profitable things is better than a lifetime filled with vanity and emptiness.**

The proud and arrogant will never make good servants and are a bad choice for leadership. They are the worst candidates for favour and blessing because they only think about themselves. If you think you can get away with being bitter and being rude to others it will bite back at you like a snake and its venom will poison you for the rest of your life, if you do not turn from it. **Beware of the nature of pride for with it comes a ruthless curse.**

Invest into your today for a lifetime of benefits by serving with the heart, firstly to God and then to man.

## THE WARRIOR IN THE STORM

If you are going through a storm in life right now, just know that God is the Creator of the winds and the clouds in the sky and so He created the storm. **The storm only lasts for a moment but the God who created the storm is eternal.** He is the Beginning and the End. So when you feel like you can't make it through your storm, **Psalms 23**, is a good scripture for you to start with. Know that God's Word will keep you through it because He is with you to the end. God never fails even if all else fails. But you have got to take a hold of God's Word with faith. **You have to be the warrior first before you can be the conqueror.** You can't have the title of a conqueror unless you have first conquered something as a warrior. The warriors of God take hold of their blessings by faith. They are undeterred and persistent in the Word. These soldiers of Christ will hope beyond hope and pursue purpose under the Shadow of the Almighty. **If your heart is set on God, no matter how great the trial you will overcome. The greater the challenge; the stronger the warrior becomes; then a conqueror is born.** When things seem impossible to bend or undo, that's when you know that you must do what you can, because *you can do it!* Don't let the circumstance steal your joy but let the circumstance be affected and changed by your joy because you are God's Warrior and Conqueror.

Take a second now and reflect on your life. If you've been battling with life's decisions, my friend, you don't have to struggle anymore because you have the real power in you. If you believe in Christ then you have His Spirit to bring you victory in all circumstances. You have the power to forgive and the power to put things right by the healing Words of the Holy Spirit in your mouth. You have the power to believe in your dream and possess what belongs to you by the purposes of God in your heart. Regardless of the thousand voices of negativity that may hinder you almost every single day, the Voice of the Holy Spirit within you is greater. Therefore, you have the power to make a change and to live an abundant life in God.

**You are worth more than gold and silver.** In reality, you own the gold and silver because your Father in Heaven is all things. Regardless of what life has thrown at you, you can choose to make a change right now even if you don't feel like it. The sooner you begin to recognise the good and respond to it with all your heart, the sooner you will begin to experience healing and transformation for your precious soul.

Choose Christ and He shall set you free. Do not be another statistic; shot down by evil. Make your name in this life through listening to the Voice of the Spirit for He alone can take you from strength to strength, and from glory to glory. God remembers those who have faith in Him. He will hear when they call upon His Name. They are His warriors, loyal to Him. They fear Him with true sincerity in their hearts. To fear God is to turn away from speaking evil and walk in the Truth (**Prov. 8:13**). Jesus said,

> *"You shall know the Truth and the Truth shall set you free."*

It will not only liberate you but also empower you and give you victory over the storm.

**(Ezek. 11:19): God wants your heart. If He can change your heart, He can change your life and everything else with it.** Do you want healing and breakthrough? Give Him your heart. Are you struggling with something in life? Let God take hold of your heart and set you into motion toward the blessing and breakthrough that you've been seeking.

**For God to enlarge your boundaries and give you your**

**heart's desires, He must first enlarge your heart by His Word.** Trust in Him and He will help you. For the strength of the LORD is more than a thousand horses and chariots (**Psa 33:16-17**). Prophet Jeremiah hits home with this truth with strong Words, saying,

> *"Thus saith the LORD; Cursed be the man that trusteth in man, and maketh flesh his arm, and whose heart departeth from the LORD... Blessed is the man that trusteth in the LORD, and whose hope the LORD is."* (**Jer. 17:5, 7**)

# CHAPTER 5

# IT'S ALL ABOUT YOU— YOU ARE PERFECT FOR YOUR SUCCESS

You are perfect for your success! By this I mean who you are and **your achievements in life are determined by your aptitude, attitude and altitude for the kind of success that you seek.** The story of your success must first be conceived in your spirit before it is revealed. It must become your vision first before it can be fulfilled. The opportunity to walk in great success can be reached by anyone who has the vision for it. The only difference is how much one has embraced the vision inside to perceive it. No matter what level or kind of success you are after this one common denominator stands; **Success is the pursuit of the heart.** If you make something of your life no one will argue with you because the fruits of success can never be disputed. But if you sit down and do nothing about the dream that God has placed in you, how can you discover the gift and power within yourself? **You are always perfect for your purpose.**

**We are all unique, and so is our path to success. The concept of success may be the same,** but the path taken will be different. Also, the training for success may be the same, but in terms of applying it, no one person is the same. Take, for example, we both can be the best Olympic swimmers and win gold medals, but our swimming style will not be the same. In light of this, you can never be someone else, even if you tried. You can only try your very best to replicate the success of high achievers and even try to be like them in the way they think and do things, but your path to success will never be the same as theirs. You will achieve your success in your way, in your own style, under your own terms and conditions, because **you are perfect for your success.** So you cannot measure yourself by another man's success because his success only defines him and not you. But you can use his success as a guide to achieve your success.

So don't be too hard on yourself if your success plan doesn't fit the picture portrayed by others. Treat yourself with the same respect that you would have others accord you and allow yourself to try and thrive amongst the best until you find your place to influence and be successful.

But if you say, *"There are others better than me."* What you are doing is measuring yourself against their success and not yours. You forget that you are not them, in likeness or image, even if you tried to. You may both want the same outcome, but how you embrace this outcome and how you get there is also not the same. You both could probably even achieve the outcome similarly, but it will not be identical at all. Thus, "similar" is acceptable, but "same" is never. Your space and capacity for success is not his space, and neither is his, yours. You are unique for your success. I do, however, encourage you to feed off the success of others and learn from their example. Grow under the sunlight and rain of success so that your roots may go deep and that you may be established in your heart and mind to flourish even in the harshest conditions. Build an appetite for your success and fill it up with your passion, learn from the best so you can walk amongst the best. You are as good as the standard you set yourself to achieve. **Try to choose only the best, follow only the best, and you will become the best.** If you don't know where to start, again, I encourage you to start with God, who alone holds the best for you in His heart and mind. If you can already perceive the fruit of your success, then it will be within your reach, with God at the centre of your pursuit. **Favour will always be with those who choose to walk with God.**

## YOUR STATUS

For me, status means to dress for your success. It means demonstrating what's really on the inside of you. It means to be in the mindset or the shoes of the person you want to become. For example, if you want to be like the richest man in the world then dress, think and feel like one. Your true status is found in your purpose. **But if you lower your inward status, then you lower your identity and credibility because no matter what colour you paint on the outside the cracks are still going to show.** If purpose determines true status, then you also learn that the higher you go the greater your success, and the greater your influence. The greater the effect you can have on others.

The question should not be, *"What do others think of me?"* But it should be, *"What do I want others to see in me that I also want for myself?"* Christ is the ultimate status that you can live and walk in

(Col. 1:27).

Don't let the world define who you are because it wasn't the world that created you but it was God who did. When the *world* defines and influences you then sin enters your life and corrupts the good things inside you. God is clear to show this in **1 John 2:15-17,**

> *"*[15] *Love not the world, neither the things that are in the world. If any man love the world, the love of the Father is not in him.* [16] *For all that is in the world, the lust of the flesh, and the lust of the eyes, and the pride of life, is not of the Father, but is of the world.* [17] *And the world passeth away, and the lust thereof: but he that doeth the will of God abideth forever."*

The status you set for yourself in your heart will be reflected outward and if Christ is in your heart, Christ will be revealed. **You must settle it within yourself that who you really are, is not what others think or say about you but what you think and say about yourself and above all what God thinks and says about you.**

## WHAT MAKES A FLOWER BEAUTIFUL?

**What makes a flower beautiful?** Before you read on to the next paragraph, pause and take a moment to answer this question for yourself. You'll be amazed by what comes out of the answer you give.

I asked my nephew one morning, *"What makes a flower beautiful?"* It took him a while to answer as he thought about why I asked this simple but strangely posed question. He knew it had to be his best three answers as per my instructions. He looked at me and said, "Uncle, the shape of the flower, the colour of the flower and the structure of the flower, by this, I mean what the flower is made of." Leaning forward with inquisitiveness, he wondered what I would say in response to his well-thought-out answer.

I looked at him with a smile, "Good answer boy! That flower is you; the way you answered this question is specific to you and has wisdom for you.

Here's why I asked you that question. Your description of the flower is the same answer you apply to your life. What kind of body-soul-spirit shape would you like to portray to others, or what is your life shaped by, what shape is it taking? Is it the shape of defeat and regret or motivation and direction? What is the shape you want?

What is the colour of your life? Be it your love life, your work life, your social life, your life in God and so forth? What kind of colour are you displaying in your life? Is it depression, bitterness and lack, or is it victory, joy, peace and love? The colour you showcase on the outside is what is on the inside of you. Have you taken the time to colour up your life? Do you think your life is colourful enough; are you happy where you are right now?

And last but not least, what is the structure of your life? You are made of power-packed elements of God: love, faith, hope, determination, courage, blessedness, peace, assurance, wisdom and knowledge. But is your structure crumbling because you lack the wisdom for a prosperous, abundant and successful life? Also, what structure are you building in your life? What is your foundation? Is it God, or is it the world?

If you have determined that these are the three main attributes of what makes a flower beautiful then you are not far from discovering what you can do to make your life beautiful. Just take the answer of the flower you gave to me and paste it into your life.

*Notice from your answer, that every flower is unique by its shape, colour and structure. So also is your life; it is unique and specially made up of its own shape, colour and structure. Want a beautiful life? Then, look no further than the lesson of the beautiful flower and apply it to your life. Like the flower, life and nature reveal wisdom waiting for us to discover and apply to our lives."*

My nephew smiled in utter amazement, "Uncle, you're really good at this! I had no clue I was about to learn a valuable lesson. Thanks uncle."

Now the answer to this question varies from person to person. Hence, the reason why I asked you to answer it before you read on any further. And the amazing fact about this is that just as all answers are unique, all flowers are also uniquely created. When I asked my wife the same question her answer was, *"You water it, nurture it and love it!"* What a good answer, and that is the answer blueprint that she can apply to her life. She must water it, nurture it, and love it with the right kind of things and the good and honourable things that God provides for her to see that beauty blossom on the inside and outside.

Again, whatever your answer is, it's a good answer because it is the obvious signal indicator that you are not far from discovering the solution and instruction to your own life's true beauty; on the inside and outside.

# CONSISTENCY

**Consistency is the key to success and mastery.** To achieve mastery in a specific art in life you must first be the 'dedicated apprentice' for that art. Consistency means steadiness, stability, persistence, determination and my personal favourite—tenacity. First things first, you are only tenacious for something if you have the vision and goals set for the outcome you desire. There is no pursuit where there is no destination or outcome. **Therefore, consistency is never without visions and goals.**

When I lived in Canberra, there was a particular woman perhaps in her sixties. She was quite obese and owned a faithful dog, which looked much like a boxer–mastiff crossbreed. One spring morning I came out to check the mail and lo before me, was this woman and her bullmastiff pacing with great intensity. I didn't think much of it but only made a mental note of it. Then every single day for three months, I would see her and her dog walking briskly around the block. She didn't miss a single morning. As the first month rolled by, I noticed her frame began to shrink. About three months later, if you were new in the neighbourhood you wouldn't have guessed that she was once used to obese. I can tell you, that woman inspired me and perhaps others, who driving by would have seen her determination and consistency.

**The Reward is yours when consistency becomes your currency and your coach.** Be consistent in all areas of your life and you will reap the benefits of your diligence. Be consistent in your love life, in your business life, in your education, in your fitness and well-being.

Let God be the head of it all and you will see the fruit of your persistence. Consistency is about the right attitude, responsibility, and work ethic in the above-mentioned areas of life. It is *dedicated effort* toward a desired outcome.

**Consistency is its own ingredient for success.** No secrets, just pure consistency. If you want something so bad, b*e consistent in* *your attitude and work ethic* for it until you reap the rewards. Consistency is one of the most important ingredients for success. Through the discipline of persistence, you will learn what to do and what not to do and develop an effective routine that results in an effective flow of events that connect to your success. Your vision and your dream require consistent attention until it is full-blown. Again, with consistency is stability, steadiness and reliability.

Ever heard of, "Practice makes perfect?" That is a true saying. Practice is consistency. Those who are consistent with their goals, will more likely than others, achieve their goals faster. **Persistence determines momentum and a good momentum results in acceleration towards success.**

**Consistency has one destination and that is success. Anyone can be successful because anyone can be consistent.** If you lack consistency in your attitude and work ethic for what you desire, you lack the stomach to handle the success that comes with it.

## DETERMINE THE OUTCOME YOU WANT

Determine the course you are going to take. It will be like Daniel's experience; though he was a foreigner, he had the upper hand. His secret of success was that HE DETERMINED THE COURSE FOR HIS HEART AND HIS LIFE. Before you pursue any goal or dream in life, whether it be a short-term, mid-term or long-term goal you must first predetermine and premeditate the outcomes you want, accept it in your heart and it is established. **Know what you want before you pursue it.** Never go on a journey without a predetermined destination. You can't go from point A to point B if there is no point B to go towards.

In addition, decide the ending to your success story and your thoughts will connect in an amazingly precise way that will lead you to that expected end. It is not an expected end intrinsically without the power of choice. That is to say, if you don't know what you want to achieve you won't know where you want to go. It's a defining point and one you must establish clearly in your mind before you attempt the journey. **Know the end of any pursuit before the actual pursuit takes place.**

This wisdom is so simple yet so powerful. **Every outcome in life is the result of what level of emphasis or attention was put behind it.** If you want something so badly, your desire for it is already the indicator that you have what it takes to achieve it. But desire alone is not enough until you make the world play your game. Harness your desires like you would harness a horse's bridle to make it turn in the direction you want it to go. When you determine the course and result of an outcome, you are saying to everything around you, that you are not here to play their game but your game. You are the best in your league and you are the one who makes the rules and determines the outcomes of the games, like a one-sided referee. **When it comes to your desires and dreams it is necessary for you to play the one-sided referee.**

## TAKE OWNERSHIP - TAKE RESPONSIBILITY

Responsibility becomes natural to you when you are the owner. Owners take good care of what belongs to them, hired employees only do what they have to do to get the job done, but owners do everything that is needed to make it a success. Albeit, you can be an employee and still have an owner's mentality for success. This wisdom or rule of life is established for every person regardless of what calibre they are in life.

Regardless of who you are you can never master an art or be successful in achieving your goals, dreams and visions until you first take ownership of what you are pursuing. Say, you love playing basketball. Do you want to be a great basketball player or *the greatest*? Then take ownership of that level of greatness and you will notice your *discipline, desire* and *determination* will automatically kick in to pursue that greatness.

Whatever is your playing field, whether it is in business, education, art or sport, you can become whatever you decide it to be. You can be great, greatest or nothing at all. A title is accorded to every form of endeavour in life. We have doctors, plumbers, builders, electricians, politicians, pastors, preachers and the list goes on. Notice all these roles require a certain level of dedication, discipline, desire and determination to achieve. Each title is a level of ownership and identity. Understand this though, **ownership always comes before identity. Discipline yourself for greatness and you will have greatness.** Train yourself for mediocrity and that's what you'll end up with. **The measure you perceive within is the measure you become.**

Can one be amongst the greats in this lifetime? Yes, it's possible! Mount Everest is a great feat to achieve. However, once the first man conquered it, many others followed. **Greatness has a *blueprint*. Follow it and you'll get there!** Know that what you seek has been achieved before and can be achieved again.

'Ownership' is a mindset. Ownership is all about taking control of one's life. It means to be comfortable in your skin about who you are and what you possess, and to simply do your best. **Only your best is needed and as you get better at doing what you love, so will your best efforts.** In doing so you increase your potential and level of aptitude for the success you are pursuing.

Much of your life's experience resulted from the decisions you made. So the first place to begin with when it comes to ownership is to correct your decisions for your life. If you have been making the same old decisions which result in the same mistakes and problems you face, it's time to change the decision to bring about the change that you are after. Taking ownership of your life means, making the choice to walk righteously, faithfully, honourably, truthfully and humbly first to yourself and then to others. **You need to prove to yourself and convince yourself that you are worth whatever it is you are pursuing.** Now dangerously if your motives are evil and you take ownership and pursue the wrong thing you will end up with every evil, violent and destructive thing that comes as a result of that unwise decision.

Do you lack joy? Then take ownership of joy; the simple rule is to accept it as a free gift, flow with it, enjoy it and reapply the same process over and over again till you overflow with it and remain in overflow mode.

Do you lack love? Then take ownership of love; simply apply the same rule again: choose to accept that you are loved and can freely give love, and you are worthy of love, receive it as a free gift, flow with it, enjoy it and reapply the same process until you overflow and remain in overflow mode.

Do you lack confidence? What are you waiting for? Take ownership of confidence; apply the same rule again: choose to accept that you can walk and live in confidence, hold your head up high, receive it as a gift without guilt, flow with it, enjoy it and reapply the process.

In all three examples of addressing *lack*, notice it requires you to make a mindset change; as I put it, delete the old mindset and install the new updated mindset. This is the mindset process of ownership. The wisdom in 'ownership' is this: *Life is hard on you because YOU are hard on yourself. But life can become easy for you if you simply do this one thing: pursue your greatness by playing your own game; letting go of the old game plan and establishing the new plan, training hard, learning smart and surely you will become great.*

**The integrity of 'ownership' is this: Ownership never plays the blame game or victim game but its own game. Never let others steal your dream, or make you feel you are not worthy of your calling.** Never let them cause you to be offended, and bitter and live in unforgiveness and hate to cause you to lose yourself. If you want the honey you will still have to put up with some bee stings. But as long as you are focused on the honey the sting must give way for you to grab a hold of that sweet honey and the honeycomb. This also means that when it comes to ownership, cutting out the unnecessary garbage and pruning yourself to blossom for your season is what it takes to be the true owner of your destiny.

Now what is the process of ownership, speaking in wisdom terms? First, you must find the game you want to play; then you must be IN the game to play the game, not as a spectator but as a player. Thirdly, you must play YOUR OWN GAME by determining what level of greatness you want to pursue. You must then learn your game, train hard and become your greatness. **Your game is your gift because in it is your greatness.**

If you let external pressures and stress decide the game you should play, then you will become a slave to that pressure and all you'll be doing is living the life you DON'T want. The phrase, "become your own boss" may sound selfish but what it really means is you get to be the one to decide what enters into your heart and what leaves your heart.

> *"Keep thy heart with all diligence; for out of it [are] the issues of life. $^{24}$ Put away from thee a froward mouth and perverse lips put far from thee. $^{25}$ Let thine eyes look right on, and let thine eyelids look straight before thee. $^{26}$ Ponder the path of thy feet, and let all thy ways be established. $^{27}$ Turn not to the right hand nor to the left: remove thy foot from evil."* **(Prov. 4:23-27)**

> *"Either make the tree good, and his fruit good; or else make the tree corrupt, and his fruit corrupt: for the tree is known by [his] fruit. $^{34}$ O generation of vipers, how can ye, being evil, speak good things? For out of the abundance of the heart the mouth speaketh. $^{35}$ A good man out of the good treasure of the heart bringeth forth good things: and an evil man out of the evil treasure bringeth forth evil things."* **(Matt. 12:33-35)**

We blame life and others but choose not to blame ourselves. **Playing the blame game will only delay your progress toward success and prosperity.** If you do not take ownership and responsibility for your own words, then your mind and heart will also follow in negligence.

Storms in life can be a hindrance to our progress and leave us cursing instead of pressing on with joy and pursuing calm waters. Hardships and challenges are there to shape you for your success. Use them as stepping stones toward success and that is how you should perceive hardship. Progress may be slow for you but if it is gradual, then eventually, you will get there if you keep going through to the end. **No momentum means 'no' growth.** Be as zealous to finish what you started because it is much easier to get something started but the true test is finishing the race. **If you are determined to finish strong, then have an attitude for a successful finish.**

## TAP ON THE SHOULDERS (POEM)

Tap on the shoulders. Direct my eyes. What may lie ahead? A storm brewing in the distant, with the lights sprinkling through the clouds.

A hoping gaze, the captain of the ship possesses. It is but the sign of a voyage soon to be fulfilled.

Hearts throb, the anchor raised. This was a ply unbridled, yet the sea welcomed

Unforeseen the eyes beheld. No craving could match but the desire of the sailor, going forth with spirit and soul.

What meets the eye is not what the heart perceives

He is gallant with the wind, the haste of the air His strength receives

Can you understand his pursuit? Can you be a part of his quest?

Innocent as the new day, as brave as the deep beneath.

Fill his cup and make merry. He captains on what no man dares trail. Wiser than owls, more valiant than lions.

His eyes light the night with a fire only the veteran can understand its secrecy

"Dance with the sea, he says." A tap on the shoulders. "Can you see what I see?"

A tap on the shoulders. "Courage my friend. We are but mere men with great hearts. This leg be the one that few desire."

"Nevertheless, that is what makes us different. We know because our hearts say so. Legacy becomes only our reward when we realise what lies ahead already belongs to us"

*Norma — Sabadi Tuesday 01- 11- 2015*

# CHAPTER 6

# GREATNESS - VISION - PURPOSE

*God does not count your failures and mistakes to bless you. Rather it is your DESTINY to be blessed in God. Therefore, with destiny is favour and blessing.*

**God does not count your failures and mistakes to bless you. God counts His purpose and calling upon you to determine your blessing.** Therefore, regardless of how many times you fail and make mistakes in life, you are made perfect for your purpose. No matter how many times you go wrong God will lead you back onto the right path. That said, God doesn't want you to live in sin. Rather, God desires that you walk upright before Him and He gives you access to progress in righteousness. The choice to do right is in your own hands.

In your heart lies the hidden map planted by God that will

show you the way to your destiny. Thus, God will give you the heart for your destiny if you will trust Him to lead you there. This truth lies in the wisdom that God created all things with a distinct purpose to fulfil. **It's not only who you are but who you will become that determines why you get blessed today. In other words, God blesses you for your destiny and prepares the path your heart should take to reach it.** Destiny will call you when things don't look right.

Inwardly, you know it's for you, even if it doesn't make sense. **Destiny will call you, *purpose* will keep you and *provision* will follow when you pursue.** God is the one who opens the pathways that will lead you to your ultimate favour and blessing. When God promises something He never breaks His promise. He is true to His Word to the end, to accomplish the purposes, which He planted in you.

The path that we walk upon, we do by *faith*. Say if someone posed a statement like, *"I don't believe in God and destiny, besides what is faith? All this faith talk is nonsense!"* How would you respond to that? Well, this is how I would respond, *"How do I know you love something like your car because we can't see love?"* It is only when you show me by your actions that I discover the intent or state of your heart and the faith by which you used to execute that intent. Just like love, *faith is substance.* **1 Corinthians 13:13** says,

> *"And now abideth faith, hope, charity (love), these three; but the greatest of these is charity (love)."*

**Hebrews 11:1** says,

> *"Now <u>faith is the substance</u> of things hoped for, <u>the evidence</u> of things not seen."*

The substance of faith is as real as the substance of love. **If you believe in God then you will receive what He has in mind for you**. Faith is the uncommon substance that possesses the uncommon reward. It is when you come to a place of absolute *belief, conviction and certainty* even when all else seems not to agree with your destiny.

The measure of our success depends on how much faith and effort we have invested in the process. What we get out of something depends on how much we put into it. There is no height too high or depth too deep that we can go. The only limit is if we believe.

**We make our demands on life when we apply our faith diligently because we know faith is of God**. Our faith can see beyond our circumstances because faith perceives through the eyes of wisdom. The Truth is *all things* should work for our good, not only because we love God, but also because we are called to fulfil a Divine purpose in our lives and that our success is specific to our calling in life (**Rom. 8:28**).

**Thus, it is our destiny that stirs the right kind of faith for the right kind of results that match us**. What you believe in points either to your destiny or away from it; that is why your faith in God is important. **Believing is seeing with the heart, because where your treasure is, there your heart will also be (Matt. 6:21)**.

For who can predict the heart of man except God who created it? **What God placed in your heart is more than sufficient to reach the destiny you were called to fulfil.**

How you perceive success is also specific to your calling in life and along life's journey your understanding of it grows. Furthermore, we define success not only by our achievements but also by the storms we have been through. You only fail when you don't get up again. Don't count your losses or failures, because they will drag you down if you focus on them constantly. But **count your victories and successes because in them lies your motivation**. If you dwell on the good things in life, they will promote and elevate you higher. Success does not depend on how many times you failed but how many times you got up and kept going. Some degree of failure came before any achievements. It doesn't matter how many times you fall, what matters is when you pick yourself up and keep pushing on.

If you're big on success remember that *time* is of the essence; use it wisely and you will find joy in your later days. Know your resources and be persistent at your goals. Mix and mingle with those who know how to produce top fruit and you will also produce top-quality fruit. **Exposure to success is the door to experiencing success itself.**

**Seek to learn from the best; seek their wisdom and it will help you find your place amongst the best**. Find yourself a mentor of success and you find yourself a good thing. You are doing yourself a favour by laying down a foundation that will last a lifetime.

A diligent man has the wisdom to build his wealth with patience, courage and confidence. Those with lazy hands are like foolish gardeners who missed the planting season and did not plant at seed time; they are like builders who built a house poorly and could not withstand the coming storm. He who builds his boat with a lazy hand and heart builds his boat to sink, not to sail. **The diligent perceive their expected result and work toward it with all their heart but the sluggish and apathetic see only what they have today and have no drive for tomorrow**. The diligent in heart will build daily with progress in his stride but the *idle* will spend most of their time worrying about tomorrow. Which one are you?

A prosperous person is not only known by his success or wealth but also by how well he was able to handle disappointments. Don't dwell on your grief because it will drain the life out of you and kill you. But dwell on the little and big victories because in them is your joy. When you have joy you have the strength to go on and succeed because true victory and success happen on the inside and those who have Christ have true victory.

**The true kind of faith finds peace even in the midst of the storm.** I woke up one morning and wrote down everything I was thankful for, and I realised I had taken for granted many blessings that God had poured into my life. You see, we are too busy worrying that we have left no time to see our prosperity and acknowledge our blessings. I have a saying,

*"Thirty seconds of peace is better than a lifetime of vanity."*

**Peace in our hearts unites our being and gives us insight and understanding to succeed; peace promotes growth.** Worry only makes the storm look bigger than it is but peace calms the storm, no matter the size. When you worry you are telling God you can handle this situation on your own. Worrying causes you to focus on the problem but joy causes you to be grateful for the solution. So when that feeling of, *"Thank God I'm alive"* comes to you flow with it and you are well on your way to where you want to be in life. Why would God give you and me a life of misery? That's not what He chose for us. He created us to live our lives to the fullest.

## YOUR GREATNESS IS FOUND IN THE GAME YOU PLAY

Life is like a game. There are winners and losers. The winners go on to become very successful. And losers, well they either remain stuck in grief or let tenacity and passion consume them so much that they become more determined than ever to go pursue victory. They use the past loss as a stepping-stone to rise to the occasion to be victors. Likewise, in the game of life, I define losers as those who let life determine their drift rather than become the cause of their greatness.

Earlier, I mentioned that your game is your gift; your gift is your greatness and that your greatness is discovered in the game you play. But **you'll never know how good you are at something if you don't have a go at it.** This is not a 'take a risk without knowledge' statement. This really is a 'discover what you can do within your own game' statement. You must first believe you have what it takes to be *great, greater* or *greatest*. That is, your game is already your vision before you even play it. The next thing of course is you've got to be in the game; play the game with all your heart, and know what you want out of it.

Play the game to discover how good you are at the game. Don't be a spectator who is only good at supporting, cheering on and commentating. If you have always just been supporting, cheering and commentating on others' visions and dreams, you are still short of the mark of the ultimate YOU. If that's all you think you are, then you're saying you don't want to be an elite, a pro, a superstar, and the grandmaster of your game. But you'd rather be lazy, mediocre, and an amateur, thus never seeking to fly. With this kind of mentality, you'll always be the kind of person settling for third best because even second best is too much for you to handle.

There will always be competition in any game you play. But if you let the competitiveness overcome you, it is because you are letting your opponents make you play their game. The challenge you face from your competitors should be the force to move you in the direction you want. If you realise this one truth that if you want to own the game you must also own the court, field or arena you play in. Your court your rules. Do you want to turn the game around? Just be good at your own game, and the game itself will fall in your favour.

Set yourself a standard and make everyone else play to that standard. You will notice this, the higher your standard, the easier the game is going to be for you. Then winning every game becomes a natural habit. **Lower your standards in life and your life will become a huge battle to overcome.** Notice that **the fruits of immorality are poor social standards and a decline in economic growth.** Do what you are good at, and you will gain not only the desired outcome; you will also receive what you are not good at.

Here's the beauty about operating this wisdom; whilst you work on being the best in your game, the game itself will begin to provide all the resources to make you greater or greatest on the inside and outside.

*Your practice is your perfection.* This is not new to your understanding, Practice! Practice! Practice! It follows the same Biblical principle of ASK and to keep asking till you receive, SEEK and to keep seeking till you find, and KNOCK and to keep knocking till the door is opened to you. **The degree of your success is equal to the amount of effort you put into playing *your* game.** Because you can produce the best effort and still lack the results because you're in someone else's game. **Greatness only comes to those who persist.**

## VISION AND THE POTENTIAL WITHIN

To discuss *potential* we must first establish this fact. 'Potential' is the knowledge and ability that exists to be utilised. **The potential within you will always be greater than what you perceive it to be.**

The knowledge you gain increases your capacity and thus increases your potential. Using knowledge for righteous purposes is wisdom from God. **The diligence of evil is destruction but the diligence of righteousness is life and peace forevermore.** You have the potential to acquire new knowledge and also the potential to succeed with it. Your success is thus equal to your potential and both are cradled and nurtured by the vision you carry within.

**Vision will never get old. Vision is forever youthful. It does not matter how old you are, you are as new as the vision you carry within.** But if you don't have vision for success, then how can you see the path before you and how do you know that you are going the right way? **If you have knowledge but no vision, you lack wisdom.** As stated earlier, wisdom is the ability to understand and apply knowledge; so **vision means seeing with your *understanding*.** Vision is important to direct the steps you should take to achieve your life's calling. Vision also releases the zeal and passion within. **Passion fixes your vision on the goal.** If you take your eyes off the prize then you will miss your reward.

Your determination to achieve causes you to focus on the

important things that you require to achieve your goal. Yet, the Lord knows every purpose under the sun and if we fix our eyes on the promises of God, He is faithful to lead us there.

Vision guides your hand to build accurately and toward perfection but no vision means no plans, no goals, no outcomes. A big vision requires a big heart and if God has given you a big vision that means you have a big heart and a lot more opportunities to succeed in life. **Never limit yourself to what you can see now as opposed to what you can have and be tomorrow because God can do more than what you think or ask.** You and I serve a God who owns the whole world. God knows not only what *you* can do, but He also knows what *HE* can do for you if you let Him. God gave me a prophetic Word for the people of God on 16 May 2013. This is what the Lord God said,

*"If you are not seeing the results you want it is because your vision is too small. **Enlarge your vision** and I (GOD) will fill it up for you and make it overflow!"*

By this, I believe what the Lord was saying is to enlarge your expectation and acceptance for a bigger vision and God will provide all the necessary resources to fulfil it. **Vision determines direction and influences progress.** Simply put, if you want it you will walk toward it. Progress comes when we have a defining moment within to understand that what we see is not the only way there, because our wise and intelligent God opens multiple ways to reach the objective. As soon as we believe in the vision we give it life to be fulfilled. **When you can see the way there, God will open all the other ways to get there.** When you initiate progress in your heart, God will release the necessary resources to help you find your treasure. **When progress finds momentum the desires of the heart are within reach.**

**You are only limited by your capacity to believe in your vision.** What separates you from the rest is the vision in you. No fuel in the car means the car cannot go anywhere. Likewise, **no desire means, no fuel for your vision.** Your passion to achieve is found in the things that matter to you. **Seek to find what makes you happy because this is where your desire and passion thrive.**

**If zeal for your vision burns in your heart like fire nothing will stop you from achieving your dream or vision.** And if Christ is your vision every other vision is secured well in Him. The value of passion produces results. It's that simple. If you have a passion for something, you will go for it. Moreover, passion is more than an enthusiastic pursuit.

**You know you have passion when you're still burning with it in the midst of disappointment and setbacks.** The fire of passion within you will burn away the *unnecessary stuff* and keep only the necessary to achieve your vision because excess luggage only weighs you down and slows progress. Know this wisdom also that **you are as good as your vision when you have developed a desire for it. Your 'potential' to achieve success lies in the vision that is conceived in your spirit.**

Enlarge your vision and God will come and fill it up. Vision without passion is like fire without heat. Passion is like a fire that grows and never gives in until you achieve your vision. The reality of your purpose in life can only be discovered once you have found the vision that keeps your heart burning. **The flames of passion within you will always point to your purpose in life.**

The power to achieve great things is embedded deep inside the heart's ability to perceive great vision by faith. **Your vision is only as real as the faith that created it.** In other words, the potential power of your faith is found in the vision you carry. **Aim to make something great and it will turn out great. Put your heart into making it the best and it will turn out extremely memorable.**

Diligence and perseverance become natural because the vision is embraced wholeheartedly. By this, I mean, that when God gives you a vision, He also gives you the hunger, and passion that is equivalent to that vision. That's why any vision conceived can be fulfilled because it is packed with the right kind of fuel for it. Hence, we can confidently say,

*"supernatural perception through the Holy Spirit delivers supernatural results ordained by God".*

**Only Heaven can deliver what no man can do.** Only God can perceive and fulfil the impossible that stands before you because all things are possible with God (**Mark 10:27**). What no one has yet seen, God has already seen for you, what no ear has yet heard, God has already heard for your sake, what no mind has yet conceived, God has conceived to fulfil in your life before He even laid the foundations of the world (**1 Cor. 2:9-16**).

God's Word to you will not pass from His eyes until He has carried out His righteous purpose in you. Hence, the Vision or Supernatural-God-Perception planted in us is summed up in these words, **"What is seen, heard and conceived in God is immutable in its nature and is destined to be fulfilled in God."**

If it is possible for God then it is possible for us who believe in God. That is why Jesus said to the man standing before Him,

*"…If thou canst believe, ALL THINGS are possible to him that believeth."* (**Mark 9:23**)

The 'impossible' can become 'possible' if you are willing to learn and discover how to make it a reality and by God, eventually bring it to fruition. Mankind couldn't fly because of his biological limitation; he was no bird and he was not created to fly. But man was given knowledge to discover flight; so he pursued on and kept learning from his mistakes and eventually discovered how he could do it. One thought led to another, and eventually, the right thought gave birth to the result he wanted. Man decided to name his new invention, an aeroplane. You know what, not only does man fly today but he flies faster than any bird you can name on the earth. **One God-thought will lead to another God-thought until a God-result is brought forth**. Then what was once perceived as impossible becomes possible and supernatural in its nature.

I, therefore, encourage you to believe in your dream and run toward it with all your heart because the truth is that you only have one life to live and one chance to make it right. It is better to go through life discovering who you are to fulfil your God-given purpose rather than to spend endless days seeking after things that do not measure up or conform to the standard of God for your life. **God made each of us unique and special for our own God-given purpose.** Only GOD is the cause and result of our faith and vision and so He alone is able to lead us to our destiny. Trust in Him and He will show you the way! **Psalms 119:105** says,

*"Thy Word is a lamp unto my feet, and a light unto my path."*

Our Father gives us all good things. **God is the direction for our desire; He is the vision for our passion and the Rewarder of our faith.** He is the music that flows from our instrument. He is the treasure of our heart and when we find Him we find the fullness of life. **James 1:5** says,

*"If any of you lack wisdom, let him ask of God, who gives to all man freely, without criticism, and it shall be given to him."*

Wisdom is God's nature and God's power conceived in us by faith and I'm talking about the kind of faith that never lets up til it achieves. With wisdom is Divine instruction to experience the glory of Christ. Wisdom is the manual for life and glory and both come from the same God. **The *Supernatural Power* of God becomes real to us when His Word becomes real on the inside of us.**

God is not far from us because He has given us His Spirit who lives in us (**John 14:16-17**). The same Holy Spirit calls out to us every day stirring our hearts toward the purposes of God for us. It is the Holy Spirit who stirs this passion in us because He is the Author of Wisdom. He is the great Teacher and the Revealer of the knowledge of the Glory of God (CHRIST). **It is the Holy Spirit who directs our faith and expectation to achieve.** The Spirit imparts to us the ability to touch the deep things of God and to experience the fullness of life. **The only thing stopping you from achieving is yourself.** When we speak of an awakening of hearts we are speaking of an awakening of passion, desire and supernatural faith in God. Only through Christ can we awake from our sleep and come out of the old nature of sin and into the life of Glory in Christ.

**When passion meets vision, and obsession touches the dream the unlimited power from within is discovered and experienced.** If you don't know where to begin, start with Christ; His *Peace*, His *Love* and His *Word*. Our quest to acquire wisdom in whatever sphere of life is really *a quest of faith, to find God first*.

Our faith is also unique to our calling. We are all given a

measure of faith to serve in the area we are called to. **Your faith is the foundation of your direction and provides the platform for your vision.** *Faith carries vision.* For faith sees and receives what the natural eye cannot see. Faith perceives the supernatural of God and leads you to the place of your blessing. **Faith through wisdom unlocks the potential in you and enlarges the boundaries of your heart.** Wisdom and faith also move your heart forward towards Godly success and not toward corruption.

Faith is a stirring in the heart. **A stirring in the heart must be adhered to because our assignment lies in the things that move our hearts.** So what is it that moves your heart? This is the clue to the purpose you are called to. You must listen to the Voice in your inner man, the Voice of the Holy Spirit within you, the Voice of wisdom and purpose calling out to you. He has been your guiding Voice to lead you on the right paths from the time you were born. Wisdom is needed to chart your course, drive your engines and steer you to your destination. You also find healing and life to your soul, health to your bones, favour to shield all your days, and knowledge to grow toward Christ. To love wisdom is to love your life enough to listen to common sense and to show respect towards the vision placed within you.

**The truth is that there is unlimited power in the Spirit of God and all it takes is your heart to discover it.** For out of the heart and mind overflow counsels of wisdom, understanding and knowledge for an abundant life. **The foundations you lay down today are important for your success tomorrow. How far you go will depend on how well your foundation was laid.** Build on the foundation of God's Word and you will never go wrong.

Now if you only go halfway with something you will receive only half the outcome you wanted. It is a simple truth and one that everyone can grasp. You don't need to be special to achieve great things. You only need to be yourself. All you need is your heart and mind to be in the right place, and God is the right place. All it takes is your simple and fervent faith in God and the rest will follow.

**Determination is a key ingredient for success.** Determination is the force, and passion is the fuel or power behind this force and the Captain of both is Jesus Christ. Jesus provides us with the vision to move forward. But you aren't your true self if you don't have the right ingredients for your vision. If you don't use the gift within you how then can you discover its many attributes?

**A gift not used is a gift wasted.** A gift not used is a story untold; a song never sung before; a portrait never painted and never enjoyed; laughter, joy and praise never shared; knowledge never revealed; a lifetime without a gift; and an opportunity never attempted and never achieved

**The greatest gift of all is salvation through Jesus Christ.** You can begin this journey of blessing by saying 'YES' to Jesus, who offers you the gift of salvation and eternal life and discover the plan He has for you. Trust that *still small voice of wisdom (Christ)* always leading you even through the hardest times.

It's time to drive this message home. I declare boldly, *"It is time for you to be the person God has called you to be! Believe in yourself. God wants you to prosper so that your fruit may glorify the LORD GOD."* Whatever is laid in your heart, that big dream that awaits fulfilment is within your own ability to achieve. **Know that God gave you the potential that equals your mission in life.** You know you can achieve it by starting now to walk toward it with confidence and determination, knowing that you have a great and loving God backing you to your success. God can give you the wisdom and the passion to fulfil the task. Now is the time to set your mind and heart to achieve. Delight yourself in the LORD God and He shall give you the desires of your heart (**Psa. 37:4**). Only trust in God and you will never go wrong. May The Favour of God be upon you, AMEN!

## REACHING YOUR HORIZON WITH VISION

*Just as there is no end to your horizons there are no limits to your possibilities.*

It's a hard climb when we can't see the top of the mountain and for some just thinking about climbing is already too hard to comprehend. However, see it this way. Every living breathing soul has a mountaintop and the same principle applies for all: the only way to get to the top is to climb upward to it. There is always new energy in us to take us a step closer to our mountaintop.

The truth is you cannot see your next horizon until you have climbed all the way to the top. Why should we climb? We should because we have a reason to. Our first and foremost reason is hidden in what lies at the top of that hill. Only you can muster the courage within to conquer your own mountain. **You alone have the formula for your own success and you do this by believing in the dream God planted in you.** If you are reckless with your desires you will only reap the fruits of your recklessness. So what is the correct way to live? To be careful for nothing but in all your ways give thanks to the Lord (**Phil. 4:6**). Trust in God with all your heart and He shall make it come to pass.

I remember working hard all day and wondering if I would get through the day alive, or that an unfortunate incident would eventually strike me down. I began to constantly pray in every moment when I felt stressed and it was in those moments that I leaned completely on God to find the ability to overcome. When my body would ache from hard work, I would sit still and watch the setting sun, take a deep breath and realise how grateful I was to see that sunset. That very sunset was beautiful because it spoke hope to me and gave me inner peace to face my tomorrow. Then, I would rise in the morning, knowing that another lot of trials and victories lay ahead of me. As much as I could, I'd give my best to keep a focused mind to get through the day. And just when I felt like giving up, I would remember that sunset and the desire to see it again kept me going till the end of the day. This became my daily vision. No matter what the day brought, I knew by God's grace I was still going to see that sunset. It didn't matter what happened to me during the day because I had found my inspiration and it was faithfully waiting for me at the close of the day. A Divine peace would surge through my being and a deep assurance would set in my heart to lift my spirit. I knew there and then everything was okay because I was in God's hands.

When that sunset passed the quiet of the night would speak to my soul to remind me to rest; that it was all well with me because God was the keeper of my soul and my song of joy in the morning. **I learnt that my faith could take me a long way if I kept encountering His peace like this.** The peace of God could take me not just another mile but hundreds of miles past the dark valley and safely into green pastures.

**I have been through many dark valleys and yet still, the peace of God prevails.** Likewise, in every heart, there is the will to survive, be free and walk in peace.

**I saw that when I had found peace at the end of each day I**

**had reached my horizon and I was ready to face the next one.** It's worth acknowledging our achievements because we use the energy created from them to propel us forward to our next assignment. Indeed, in life, we go from one horizon to another, from strength to strength and glory to glory with Christ by our side.

Failure and mistakes make our hearts sad. But you are not a failure if you keep trying. You may fail from many attempts but if you are persistent one day you'll finally get it right. Failure is defined by our current shortfalls so it is not a good measure of the full potential one may possess. However, failure should be seen as a learning curve to make you better at your game. **Our gifts and talents are cultivated through both failure and achievement.** In other words, it is through failing that we discover our strength to succeed and with every victory we grow stronger.

**Your talent is where your heart is; your gift to bless this world is also there. Find it and you find your power to succeed in life.** The gift within you will bring you before men and women of great status and wealth (**Prov. 18:16**). Our success is thus, measured by how far we have gone to make it work. If we go halfway we get a half baked result. If we nurture our little achievements with the right kind of wisdom we are bound to reap pleasant rewards in the hundred-folds. You may find this hard to believe, but **where you currently are shows how much you have challenged yourself to get to your mountaintop.** I wrote this not to discourage you but to make you see that you are not yet there and must keep going till you reach the top. You must reach your horizon so that you can look beyond to the next horizon. The end of one horizon begins another. **Just as there is no end to your horizons there are no limits to your possibilities.** The possibilities towards a successful life are endless and they are also achievable with God by your side.

The only thing required is to take one step at a time, place one foot before the other, till you reach your horizon. The moment we stop planning for success we become stale and too comfortable that we allow ignorance and complacency to lead us into the wrong path. Going down the mountain sounds easier but it will never lead you to your mountaintop. There is only one way to the top and it is upward.

**Ambition without goals is like having eyes without vision. A mentor with vision is better than a leader without direction;** because **vision is direction**. And every great journey is achieved with little steps. **The biggest dreams are achieved in chunks of little victories and achievements.**

Your vision points to your purpose. Don't let your current circumstances steal your vision from you. When your heart is set on progress all you see is your vision recreating, evolving and refining itself to become better every time you replay it, thus leading you to take the next step forward. **Your vision then becomes your mentor, coach and guide to show you the way.**

**The Word of God also provides profound vision for you.** The Holy Spirit can impart wisdom and vision to us when we abide in His Word. God's Word is much more ancient than ancient itself because it is the Beginning and it is more modern than tomorrow because it is the End. Even our current day science is still too young to perceive because really what science is, is the discovery of the infinite wisdom and knowledge of God. Hence, when we are guided by His Word, wisdom comes alive in us and brings forth clear direction and vision to guide us on into the right path (**Psa. 25:4-9**). Perceive life through the eyes of God's wisdom and not by your own sight. By sight, I mean living selfishly only for today. When we focus only on today we limit ourselves; we become greedy and forget that there is blessing that exists for everyone's tomorrow. **When you're selfish about today, you'll worry about tomorrow. However, if you're generous about today, tomorrow will take care of itself.** Because of selfishness, we become tunnel-visioned and see only one horizon before us.

But God's wisdom sees unlimited horizons of opportunity ahead. God wants to lead you into green pastures and beside quiet waters. He has given us His Word to be a lamp onto our feet and the light onto our path (**Psa. 119:105**).

Success is all about personal growth and development. Success is not static but progressive in nature. So it must be maintained and developed constantly.

By this, I mean reaching one objective is the beginning of another. If you can't take the first step you can never discover beyond yourself. If vision means the way up then you should go towards it. Don't be held back, you are better than what you think you are. Because the vision that you bear will not pass until it is fulfilled in your life. For **God is faithful in every generation.**

## VISION AND GOAL PLANNING

Your vision is your mento. It is good to plan your goals and follow your plan but it takes vision to direct your goals. When your plan fails, plan again and keep planning till you succeed as success is never achieved in vain but with deliberate focus.

When you walk with vision you are bound to succeed. **Plan imaginatively and realistically and your goals will be reachable**, that is, small steps eventually get you there to the big one. Yes, one step at a time means one step closer to the ultimate goal. **Realistic goals mean real achievements and real outcomes which reward your time, your efforts and your energies.** Your goal can only be as real as your vision. This is good for you in that it motivates you and moves you in the direction you want to go. **Achieving small goals should be your game strategy and game changer.** A good illustration of this is like building a 100-floor skyscraper. To build the 100th floor we must first build the other 99 floors to get to it.

Your small successes should boost your confidence and morale to not only survive to the end but come out fighting with more strength than when you first began, and drive you to your ultimate prize. As you go higher in your goal setting, more *time* is needed to wait, plan and execute to achieve this goal.

Also in many instances, it may take longer to plan but shorter to execute. **Perfect planning brings perfect results.** With that said, there is no limit to your ability to achieve if you plan well for it. You could achieve a big goal in one day if you choose to and it all depends on how well you have planned for it. The power to choose and change your life is in your own hands. That's the beauty of dreaming and then setting out to achieve. Do you want to be successful? Then plan toward it with passion. Plan with wisdom and understanding; plan with your head and heart planted in God's Word and your path will always have a light to lead you on. **Psalms 119:105** says,

*"Thy Word is a lamp onto my feet and a light onto my path."*

**Know that the master plan of destiny never fails if you are in Christ. When your plan fits God's plan, He will bring it to pass.** Be confident in your plan and you will get there. The good thing is that plans are made to be flexible so you can adjust and refine them as you go along. Surely there is always a level of risk-taking when it comes to planning. **Don't be afraid to take risks if you can see your breakthrough but never let your risk-taking affect others negatively.**

## YOU ARE DESTINY AND PURPOSE

*"Before I formed you in the belly I knew you. And before you came forth out of the womb I sanctified you, and I ordained you a prophet unto the nations."* **(Jeremiah 1:4-5)**

God never made a mistake when He called and ordained us to bear fruit (**John 15:16**). **God does not make mistakes. He knows whom He has chosen and called and what they will do in life.** We live for some-thing greater than ourselves. Our gain is the blessing of others.

**You can do everything in your power to be different but real power comes from God to be different.** My dad would always say to me, *"Just be yourself, son, just be you, the way God made you. Because the way God made you is perfect to fulfil your calling and destiny."*

I began to understand this in a much deeper way, that you best be yourself to discover what you are capable of achieving. **Find your place to be yourself and you find your rhythm for life.** No one can deny you of your uniqueness. No one person has the same abilities, only similarities.

You are unique for a reason: that you may discover the different colour of wisdom set for only you. Thus, being yourself is important for your success because only you can achieve all your dreams and fulfil the purpose that God has planted in you. Destiny will always have the last say. Your purpose is a seal upon your life by the Spirit of God, which can never be undone. If God is your guiding light you will never lose your way.

The big question is, how will I know if I have finally found my purpose in life? When you have finally found your calling in life, the words, *I was born for this* will make real sense to you. Our LORD Jesus summed it up in these Words,

> *"...Thou sayest that I am a king. To this end was I born, and for this cause came I into the world, that I should bear witness unto the truth. Everyone that is of the truth heareth My voice."*
> **(John 18:37)**

**You are destiny and purpose.** No one can tell you what it is, nor can they find it for you. Only you can! The feeling of knowing your purpose is so peaceful that you fear nothing. You feel you are finally at home, you have finally found your beginning and one that speaks your completeness within. You find joy flowing out of you. **That place of purpose becomes your holy moment where even time seems to have stopped to acknowledge you.** Every other thing you do in life will be drawn to fulfil your main purpose; because you have finally discovered your art and mastered it. To you, this is your zone. It describes and defines who you are. It is **your true call of duty—what you would passionately lay down your life for**. When you are finally there you begin to move fluently with it, without stalling.

**You pick up momentum and you become powerful in your own arena as the LORD leads you on. Human flaws become secondary when your heart has found its perfect place.** You are the man or woman of your moment and you become the picture of completeness; the example of resilience and hope and the inspiration for all those who follow behind. When you have finally found your calling in life never let God out of the picture. Make Him the centre of it and you will never go wrong. You have finally found your mountaintop and the real journey has begun for you. Many more horizons now await you to conquer as the master of your destiny.

Stand strong like Joshua (**Josh. 1:3-9**) and run the rest of the way with God by your side.

## THE LEADER - THE MAN OF PURPOSE

*The man of purpose sees the goal and he runs to it.*
*His heart is focused on the result.*

**A man of purpose, is not defined only by what he authors but also by what he finishes**; for the true winner is the one that finishes the race. The true man of purpose will never buckle until he finishes what he first started. And that is what it means to finally find one's treasure, and the treasures of the heart are never far off.

**A leader has vision and the valiant spirit to follow what he sees.** A leader is one who has knowledge and skill to fulfil what he pursues. Purpose is always the name of his game. The spirit of a leader is like a fresh new day filled with new strength and new direction. In the Leader is fulfilment and peace just like the sunset. For in the toughest of times a leader will always stand out. His energy is exuberant and influential in that wherever he goes so does his powers to influence with him. He is an effective leader and his words are for progress and purpose, and for healing and blessing so that those who hear him find direction and inspiration to keep them on the right path.

**A leader with vision is a strong man in the house of God.** A strong man upholds the standard and keeps the pace for everyone else to follow. He is like one of the pillars in the house with Jesus as the main CornerStone. **Jesus calls us to be leaders when it comes to possessing our ordained blessings.** A true leader initiates the process of purpose because his sight is set on the outcome of that process. All purposes that lead to a great harvest of peace and wholeness in Christ Jesus are ordained by the LORD.

If one day you wake up to find your leader is no longer there for you, it will quickly dawn on you that you must be the leader of your own destiny. **Be the initiator of God's purposes and you are on your way to becoming an excellent leader.** Why leadership? *It is because your purpose needs mentorship and good leadership to get you there.* If you cannot own your purpose, no one else will until you awake to fill the shoes of your own calling. You must become the leader of your own purpose and destiny; seek it till you find it, and the best place to start looking is *GOD*.

Wisdom Calls Out To You

# CHAPTER 7

# THE TRUE POWER OF EXPECTATION

*"For thus saith the Lord...I will visit you and perform my good Word toward you, in causing you to return to this place. [11] For I KNOW the thoughts I think toward you, saith the Lord, thoughts of peace and not of evil, to give you an expected end. [12] Then shall ye call upon me, and ye shall go and pray unto me, and I will hearken unto you. [13] And ye shall seek me and find me when ye shall seek me with all your heart."* **Jeremiah 29:10-13**

**Expectation is the mother of opportunity and the carrier of the potential to succeed.** Expectation will bring you to the doors of opportunity but it is your words of faith that will unlock those doors. **Expectation carries the initiatives to do mighty exploits for the LORD.** Expectation encourages the progress of wisdom because **wisdom is the master scientist of every witty**

invention and holds the master key to every door of blessing. Expectation pursues the result and seals the deal. **A nation is born out of expectation for success and prosperity that is why expectation is the mother of opportunity. Expectation grooms the heart to be strong and builds resilience in a warrior.**

**Expectation guides the hand of a teacher and the vision of a mentor. Expectation creates great leaders.** It is the main motivator behind every great event because there is vision and purpose within. It is more than the key element of thought process because it is involved in every decision we make. In the bosom of expectation in God, is faith and hope and its roots are founded on the resilient love of God.

God knew His thoughts were directed toward you and me. His thoughts were of peace and prosperity for us and to give us an *expected end*.

This is the ultimate form of expectation we can lean on knowing also that nothing can separate us from the love and purposes of God (**Rom. 8:38-39**). Isn't that amazing? You were purposed for good things even before you were born. The phrase *'expected end'* is sort of like the parking space of Mr. Purpose, the Senior Executive of the administration department of Heaven. Purpose dwells in God's Throne. 'Purpose' is born of God. **God breathes and speaks purpose**. When God spoke purpose into existence for you, He had an expectation for it to do what it was purposed to do. Thus, expectation is like the *sole* to the *foot* of faith and purpose.

**Expectation through opportunities steers you to your purpose.** Expectation is the energy and drive behind desire. It brings all your focus into one place with laser-like precision so that you can achieve great feats and become the master of your destiny. If our expectation is aligned with God's expectation of us then we have found our true purpose in Him. When one begins to seek God with all their heart the clutter of life is cleared out and all their attention is zeroed in on God. The resilient nature of faith is coupled with expectation. Faith is never without expectation because our faith is enhanced by expectation. **Expectation lives and breathes for the result. It possesses supernatural perception that produces a desired outcome without fail.** It is the mentor to great men and women of faith. True expectation is never with- out diligence. **Expectation coupled with diligence produces pleasant results.** It is that *faith with diligence* which pleases God (**Heb. 11:6**). **God's favour is our power to prosper.** If God chose to turn His back on us not even our own efforts will help us succeed.

The woman with the issue of blood in **Luke 8:43-48** had an expectation for her healing and she did not back down until she touched the edge of Christ's garment. I like how it reads in the book of
Matthew;

> *"And, behold, a woman, which was **diseased** with an issue of blood twelve years, came behind Him, and touched the hem of His garment:* <sup>21</sup> ***For she said within herself, If I may but touch His garment, I shall be whole.*** <sup>22</sup> *But Jesus turned Him about, and when He saw her, He said, Daughter, be of good comfort; thy faith hath made thee whole. And the woman was made whole from that hour."* (**Matt. 9:20-22**)

> *"Then touched He their eyes, saying, According to your faith be it unto you."* (**Matt. 9:29**)

Faith and expectation are spiritual things. And both virtues operate in the realm of God's grace and love.

Therefore, expectation is the direct link between what you receive (your desired outcome) and the faith it took to receive it! Expectation connects your faith to your desired outcome.

Faith that operates with expectation will produce a constant flow of results. God wants the best for you so you should also pursue only the best for yourself. **Your goal is God's gold and God's goal is your gold**. Your expectation will position you for the results you want. So **if you really want to do, be and have something, position yourself for it by faith**. Also, our Faith with expectation causes us to delight in God. We can find this truth in **Psalms 37:4** which says,

*"Delight thyself also in the LORD; and He shall give thee the desires of thine heart."*

Anyone can produce a hundred-fold fruit over and over again if they can understand this simple truth that there are only limits but no limitations in God. By this I mean, we may have a limit to how much we know and ask for but there is no limit to what God can do for us.

*"But as it is written,* ***Eye hath not seen, nor ear heard, neither have entered into the heart of man, the things which God hath prepared for them that love Him.****"* **(1 Cor. 2:9)**

*"Now unto Him that is able to do exceeding abundantly above all that we ask or think, according to the power that worketh in us."* **(Eph. 3:20)**

# CHAPTER 8

# RAISING A STANDARD AGAINST THE ENEMY

*"So shall they fear the Name of the LORD from the west, and His Glory from the rising of the sun. When the enemy shall come in like a flood, the Spirit of the LORD shall lift up a standard against him."*
**Isaiah 59:19**

## FROM DRYNESS TO ABUNDANCE

**Changing from one decision to the next is a transition.** Moving houses is a transition. A change in the weather is a transition. Going from dryness to abundance is a transition. The sun rises in the morning and sets in the evening, that's transition. **With every level of decision is a transition** from buying the weekly groceries to keeping the exercise schedule, to paying the bills. *Choice is change and change means transition.* Life is full of transitions. If everything around us is constantly experiencing change, then we ourselves must also become transitional and adaptable to changes that promote our growth, our wellbeing and our breakthroughs. Transitions are sometimes painful and uncomfortable. However, to push through the clouds is to see the sun and the clear sky. This allows us to see a greater and better view of things. Transition means finding the right set of keys to the door of your next level of blessings.

For the Israelites to leave Egypt they had to Cross the Red Sea of their *transition* from bondage to freedom. Then for them to enter into the Promised Land filled with milk and honey, they had to cross the River Jordan, representing their *transition* from the dryness of the desert into the abundance of the Promised Land. It is the same with you and me.

For us to enter into our breakthroughs and blessings we need to cross a transition, which will depend on the *spiritual decision* we make. If we walk in the Spirit we will move forward to our promise. But if we walk in the world we will go backwards again to bondage, slavery to sin, and the powers of darkness. If you are not yet free of these powers, Christ can set you free. All you have to do is give Him your heart and He will fill you up with His Spirit and lead you to your Promised Land.

There is one thing that remains undefiled and that is the *Word of God*. **When the highest Word from God is given, nothing but faith and obedience is needed**. I find two important points in this statement. Firstly, **God's Word will bend any situation to fulfil its purpose (Isa. 55:11)**. And secondly, faith gives God a reason to act. I ask you this question. Is there a Word in your heart today stirring your faith and prompting you to act? A prompting from the Spirit is like waters ready to burst forth.

But let's get down to the heart of this truth. The real question here is *what are you attracting into your life?* Is it the right thing for you? Is it worthy of you? Is it worthy of praise? Is it worthy of good virtue? Does it make you happy? Will you have regrets if you have it? Does it serve to bless others? Will it bring you blessings for your future? And the most important question to ask; *is God in it?*

## THE POWER OF GRATEFULNESS

Look to Heaven, and release that overflow of thanks and praise within. The weapon of *appreciating* and *acknowledging the goodness of life* will bring you from dryness into abundance. Are you in some sort of dryness and your walk with God has become dull? Thankfulness is your key for breakthrough. If you are struggling to *praise* God, start with being *grateful* and the doors of opportunity will burst open to receive you. **Any thought that encourages dryness is bondage on your life, and thankfulness can break these mental blockages.**

**Gratefulness will give you joy, and joy leads to the heart of God** (Psa. 100:4-5). Gratefulness in your heart comes from humility and humility pleases the LORD. **Gratefulness will teach you to appreciate what you have and it will also open your heart to greater things.** There is nothing too big or small for God.

He can bring us from a place of dryness into abundance but we must always have a thankful heart toward God if we are to receive from Him direction to walk into our promise of abundance. As I noted earlier in this book; *the beginning of good stewardship is thankfulness.*

# THE VANTAGE POINT

*Little is known of a man when he goes through trials and temptations because everyone goes through them. But great is known of him when he endures and overcomes them. This then is **The Vantage Point**.*

The quote above voices the same wisdom found in **James 1:12**. Evil finds its power to lure you in temptation so that it will draw you away from the Truth of the Spirit. **Weakness saps confidence out of the heart but courage gathers the heart for victory.**

**We always try to put our best foot forward but God knows the other one too.** We continuously strive to conceal our unfavourable spots whilst we search to find the strength we need to overcome the secret sins in the hidden places of our heart. So you are not alone in the quandary of temptation. God knows and He can deliver you and give you the strength you need to overcome. When you fail to overcome a temptation, do not drown yourself in guilt, regret and sorrow but surrender yourself to the Lord completely. Don't settle with defeat and make a deal with *sin*, because the truth is that you are a new creation in Christ Jesus and that the Spirit dwelling in you has greater power to overcome and make you more than a conqueror.

The devil doesn't want you to know the Truth of Life in Christ Jesus, but **If you are diligent, your weaknesses will make way for strength; your insecurities will surrender to favour and your heart will be clothed with power from the Holy Spirit.**

Christ did not waste His time when He died on the Cross, He was diligent and fully surrendered to the Holy Spirit and the Will of the Father right up to the Cross of our Salvation. He paid the ultimate price with His life that you might walk free from the chains of sin, bitterness and temptation and enter in the fullness of life in the Spirit of God.

All you have to do is surrender to God as Christ did. For those who are in Christ, who walk after the Spirit, are no longer condemned. Walk toward Christ Jesus, the Captain of our Salvation. Christ came to set you free from the corruption of sin. **A corrupted truth is already a lie because it is truth mixed with a lie, which produces nothing but confusion**. If your conscience tells you that you are defeated, surrender it to Christ and watch Him transform your mindset into a warrior and victor. He'll soak you with pure truth and life. God has given us the Holy Spirit of Truth. The same Holy Spirit is the Spirit of power, love and sound mind to overcome all temptation (**2 Tim. 1:7**).

If only you would realise this, that no one is perfect including myself and that the sooner you realise this, the better it will be for you to get up each morning and see each day as an opportunity to go out and achieve your dreams and goals with the grace that Christ overshadows us with. If dreams and goals were easy to achieve, there would be no challenge and no real victories to celebrate. There would be no valiant spirit to acknowledge, or endeavour to overcome. That said, in this world of imperfection God sees you differently; those who have surrendered their all to Christ, you are already perfect in Christ and all you have to do is accept this state of mind and become the vessel of honour that Christ ordained you to be. **Live in the power of grace and walk by the power of grace.**

Jesus said it in simple but firm words when His forgiveness and mercy showed greater courage against those who were about to stone the woman accused of adultery. He said to her,

*"Go and sin no more"*

Christ wasn't just saying to the woman to stop sinning, but that she needed no more to be bounded by the sin and guilt and failure of this flesh but free in the freedom of Christ and remain free.

Here's a list of the types of temptations that we face today. If you recognise any of these in your life, now would be the right time to surrender it to the Lord of Glory, experience the power of His Spirit and freedom within:

- The temptation of *pride* seeks to destroy every good thing you build. Pride destroys your grounds for blessing and prosperity and blinds your vision from seeing beyond yourself. **Pride is a type of crippling fear in disguised in selfishness.**
- The temptation to be *deceitful and selfish* comes from our attempt to try to fill a void of emptiness or acceptance by trying to gain without being considerate for others. Selfishness only pleases itself and not God.
- The temptation of *power* seeks to divert us from our true course that leads to our destiny and makes us slaves of the devil and not Christ. By power, I mean the authority to make decisions in favour of truth. Power seekers don't pursue truth, they pursue selfish gain and deceit, and fame at the expense of others. A leader blinded by selfish pursuits is like a smoke about to vanish in the wind with no good thing to remember him by.
- The temptation of *unforgiveness* poisons us with bitterness, anger and hate so we become slaves of darkness and bring a curse upon ourselves.
- The temptation of the *flesh* will frustrate our good intentions to walk with the LORD and to focus on progress. Instead, the flesh deceives us with a cloud of

doubt and strangles us with its lusts to hold us down, rather than move forward. Sadly, we become enslaved by its crippling hold.

To sum it up, what really is the *Vantage Point*? It is surrendering your all to Jesus.

Sin is a path toward death, a trail of darkness, regret and shame. We were lost in it and it was for this reason that God sent Jesus, He's only Son to save us from death.

There is also the path of Life-in-Christ. The path of sin is wide and easy to the flesh, but **the path of Life-in-Christ is narrow, yet full of the might of the Holy Spirit, for those who surrender to God**. Are you willing to surrender your heart to Jesus, if you haven't yet, Jesus invites you to experience the victory, freedom and hope that is in Him, it's a dream and a miracle birth within His Spirit for you, and it will become yours the moment you say,

> *"Jesus I surrender my heart to you. Come and be Lord of my life."*
> *"[Christ] Who in the days of His flesh, when He had offered up prayers and supplications with strong crying and tears unto Him [the Father] that was able to save Him from death, and was heard in that He feared;* [8] *Though He were a Son, yet learned He <u>obedience</u> by the things which He suffered;* [9] *And being made perfect, He became the author of eternal salvation unto all them that <u>obey Him</u>;"* **(Heb. 5:7 – 9)**

# THE PRIDEFUL HEART

*"The fear of the LORD is to hate evil: pride, and arrogancy, and the evil way, and the froward mouth, do I hate."* **Proverbs 8:13**

*"A man's pride shall bring him low: but HONOUR shall uphold the humble in spirit."* **Proverbs 29:23**

My prayer is that, as I uncover the *spirit of pride* to you, that you will also take the time to look into your own heart and may be if you notice a hint of pride, that will not hold back but surrender it to God. God is abundant in grace and He wants to touch your heart as you will His.

The *spirit of pride is a blind leader* and those who follow it are lost in deep darkness. Often pride doesn't have a tag because no one really wants to claim it as theirs, just so they can feel pure within themselves. But the pride-in-the-heart that I speak of is the one that is not willing to surrender to God and the Spirit of God.

Pride will make you look inward to satisfy only what you want but not outward to be considerate of others. **Pride is stubbornness and rebelliousness against God's Voice.**

**Pride only talks about itself. Those caught in it hope to paint a better picture of themselves before others rather than be honest. When the arrogant man boasts openly about himself he is already showing that he lacks wisdom and the fear of God.** Pride only considers what makes it happy, even if it hurts someone else. **Pride is utter selfishness and creates strife and division among family and friends.**

Years that could have been spent caring and loving are lost in disputes because of high-mindedness. Pride speaks evil of others and is riddled with jealousy and cunningness to destroy. The words of his mouth may sound sweet but he is void of truth, peace and sincerity that comes from deep within a true humble heart. Pride lacks true wisdom. Its tongue is like a poisonous snake that spits out venom. When a person is blinded by pride, they don't realise that the pit they dug up to set as a trap for others is the same pit they will fall into.

> *"For all that is in the world, the lust of the flesh, and the lust of the eyes, and the pride of life, is <u>not</u> of the Father, but is of the world. <sup>17</sup> And the world passeth away, and the lust thereof: but he that doeth the will of God abideth forever."* (**1 John 2:16-17**)

Pride is not of God, it is evil and dark in all its forms. Pride is an abomination to God and those who love a prideful life are blinded by it. Pride makes the heart cold and hard. The heart of pride is neither able to receive nor understand advice as pride is void of wisdom and is filled with the foolishness of the world. *Arrogance* does not understand the ways of God. Hence, it cannot inherit the blessings that come from God. **Anything that opposes Christ has pride attached to it.**

**The conceited think they are right in all their ways that is why there is no point in arguing with them.** Do not try to argue with an arrogant person because all you will get are stones of negativity and bitterness hurled at you. Walk away from the fool and maybe he will finally understand what you are trying to get across to him.

A prideful heart thinks it is perfect but perfection only comes from God. Pride is full of flaws; it is of the flesh and the devil, therefore it cannot inherit the things of the Spirit of God. **Those who claim to be God's and yet live a life lost in the corruption of the world make themselves liars before God and before man.**

Their corrupted hearts deceive them into thinking they are doing good for themselves but they have been fooled by the jealousy and bitterness that grips their hearts, blinds their eyes and deafens their ears to Life found in the Spirit of Christ. Pride respects no man because it is evil in its nature. Arrogance loves destruction and wickedness. It is deceitful and cunning. **Pride will never initiate peace but would rather choose aggressive exploits for its own gain. Pride does not know the ways of God.**

But **the true peacemaker is the one who initiates the process of peace**. The conceited heart will inherit the wind because he chooses to stir up trouble and division **(Prov. 11:29)**. **If you think you have humility but still hold unforgiveness within, you are actually still in your pride because** *unforgiveness is pride.* True forgiveness will set you free and release within streams of living waters that will overflow. *Forgiveness brings forth true worship to God.*

Let Christ's light shine through you. Be a true representative of Christ and hold on to peace and humility. Be truthful and honest to an arrogant person. In doing so you might save their soul from the pit of destruction. This pleases the Father in Heaven who sees everything we do and He will reward us according to what is in our hearts.

Oh you righteous! Do not throw your precious gems to the arrogant, for the eyes and ears of their hearts have been shut by pride and selfishness. They are like pigs without understanding that only trample on your good deeds and good words and instead attack you with hasty anger, jealousy and bitterness. The wicked are filled with their vile ways, they seek to swiftly destroy the righteous but violence and destruction will be their reward in the end because *God will defend the righteous in his cause.*

Pride will try to tear you down with his words and he finds pleasure in doing this but he himself is a lost cause. Have nothing to do with him. Do not even borrow a single thing from him because all he will do is mistreat you in the end. Instead of being kind, he will hate you even more. We as God's children must use God's wisdom. We must sternly rebuke the arrogant about his attitude because it is his salvation. Yet we do this out of love and concern for him. If you correct the prideful man, he will either hate you for it or he will accept your correction and have a change of heart.

*Wisdom has a way of even unlocking the heart, even that of the stubborn and making him submit.*

Only God's Word can cut deep through soul and spirit and is able to cut through the thickness of pride and rescue a soul (**Heb. 4:12**). Yes, the Words of wisdom are like life-giving waters that can save and redeem souls.

**It is better to offer the message of life to the arrogant than to feed him with what he wants to hear.** The arrogant is void of understanding neither is judgement found in his heart. But the humble know the way of judgement and walk with a discerning heart.

If you think you are humble then you must hear both sides of any argument before you can pass judgement. You must be willing and patient to support the cause of peace because in any argument no story is true until it is weighed out by the virtues and wisdom of God.

Do not be envious when the wicked boast about their prosperity. The truth is their foundations are unsteady; built on lies and deceit and will not last. They will vanish like smoke in the wind (**Psa. 73**).

Speaking the truth is better than telling a lie to try to win the approval of man. **The one who tells a lie is laying traps for his own soul. His own tongue will become his betrayer leaving him with great grief and regret.**

There is a way to rebuke and correct the mistakes of others and it is not in pride. **Do not accuse or judge others harshly with loud words in public so as to humiliate them and crush their soul.**

Remember, **the venom of evil words is from the pit of hell and a tongue that speaks wickedly without hesitation is void of the honour of God but possesses the nature of a deadly snake.** Let your kindness and compassion protect and embrace others. In doing so, you will win their respect and bring on yourself great honour and favour. Address the mistakes of others in secret, where no eyes or ears are near. If you do this they will learn to grasp wisdom early and turn to the paths of life. **Respect rewards respect, and honour rewards honour. If you forcefully try to gain respect you are like bitterness in the belly of those whom you offend.** You will only be vomited out, called names and made an outcast.

**Respect is cultivated through humility.** It is better than the praise of men. Humility without respect is false humility. The knowledge of the arrogant only produces more foolishness because they lack the capacity to listen with their hearts. The true fear of God is to keep from doing and speaking evil (**Prov. 8:13**) but pride refuses instruction because it feeds on evil conversations and evil schemes.

The one who schemes evil against others is cursed and will drink the venom of his cup. **It is foolishness to desire evil for others and think that you are safe. Evil shall hunt the violent man and overthrow him (Psa. 140:11).** God seeks righteousness and humility but He abhors pride (**Isa. 66:2**). The devil, filled with pride in his heart, tried to exalt himself above God but God threw him out of glory and condemned him to the lake of fire. So repent of your conceited ways or you will end up like the devil and be cursed with an eternal curse from God.

**Living with an arrogant man is like living next door to a dry and empty desert and even if his waters flow it produces only bitterness which no one can drink.** But living with a humble person is like living beside the calm waters of life; they are refreshing to anyone who takes a drink from them. But be warned, if you take advantage of the humility and hospitality of others to satisfy the corruption in your heart, God Himself will come to their defence and stand against you and no one survives a battle against God.

**Limitations come when we are full of pride and ignorance.** By this I mean. When God shuts a door on you, it's because he doesn't want you to be caught up in the mess that is about to cripple you or that you are already in. He takes you through the valley of the shadow of death so he can show you life and honour on the other side of it. God wants you free from the grip of sin. He wants you to see that in Christ there are no limit but freedom in the heart. The moment we let pride and ignorance sit in our heart, we deprive ourselves from experiencing the true blessing in God. **To abide in righteousness is the comfort of the upright in heart, but it is sickness to the arrogant.**

Pride is covetousness, or being full of oneself. The LORD hates greed or *covetousness* (**Psa. 10:3**) because greed leads to falsehood or lies. Selfishness seeks its own ways and refuses to hear the Voice of the LORD (**Jer. 6:9-19**).

Therefore, **the heart of a ravenous man is his own downfall because he seeks only to please himself at the sacrifice of others,** even if it means to destroy them. His heart will seek to do what it wants without shame or remorse. **The greedy man is like the taste of bitterness on the tongue and sickness to the body.** His greed is his curse and if he does not repent of it, this curse will pass down to his children and their children's children. What a dreadful reality for those who decide to become selfish in their ways. Greed also stirs jealousy. Stay away from greed and selfishness. **Those who are consumed with greed have a void they cannot fill.** Even the gates of hell are not far from their heart and their path leads to total destruction.

# CHAPTER 9

# FORGIVENESS: FIND HEALING FOR YOUR SOUL

*Forgiveness is a key principle of the Kingdom of God.*

Before we delve into the topic of forgiveness let us look at some related scriptures to see what the Word of God says about forgiveness and offence:

> *"A brother offended is harder to be won than a strong city: and their contentions are like the bars of a castle."* **Proverbs 18:19**

> *"For if ye forgive men their trespasses, your heavenly Father will also forgive you:* [15] *But if ye forgive not men their trespasses, neither will your Father forgive your trespasses."* **Matthew**

**6:14-15**

Many who read the **Matthew 6:14** verse often ask, *'how can God not forgive? Isn't He a forgiving God?'* Yes, God is the Author of Forgiveness. However, in this scripture, God is also faithful to His spoken Word and once He has declared it He cannot go back on it (**Num. 23:19-20**). In this passage God is laying down the principle or the wisdom of forgiveness which He Himself cannot alter. *There is no unforgiveness in God and there is no unforgiveness in Heaven.* So those who harbour unforgiveness are certain to miss out on Heaven. **You can do all the right things in the world and even serve the LORD faithfully but the bile of unforgiveness will deny you the right to enter into your inheritance in Heaven.** Why is this? Because unforgiveness is bitterness and pride that bind the heart in darkness, and God knows the condition of every heart, even yours.

You might argue and say, *"But I have accepted Christ in my heart and isn't Jesus the way to the Father?"* Yes, you speak the truth but **Jesus Christ, the Son of God, did not come to be an example of unforgiveness but of forgiveness.** In fact, on the Cross from which He hung He uttered one of the most powerful words ever, *"Father, forgive them for they do not know what they are doing."* And Jesus commands us to *go and do the same* (**Luke 10:37**). Even through His suffering and torment, instead of cursing His accusers He prayed to the Father to forgive them. He overcame the darkness of bitterness by the light of forgiveness. Christ did not just preach forgiveness He lived forgiveness even up to the point of death. Here we see that **forgiveness is a key principle of the Kingdom of God.** God has spoken this principle into existence through Jesus Christ. If you cannot forgive those who have offended you, how then can you expect forgiveness from God our Father?

## THE PRIDE OF UNFORGIVENESS

**Unforgiveness is a form of pride and pride in the heart is sin.** Pride and sin cannot enter Heaven. Neither can pride and sin commune with the LORD GOD.

Are you fighting amongst yourselves? Know that arguments expose the inner hurt and bitterness of unforgiveness harboured in the heart. Just hear the conversation of two individuals who have hurt each other with their words. The weight of unforgiveness can cause a person to hate and even kill; to their crippled heart, they have measured the offence committed and declared vengeance rather than peace.

**Forgiveness is much more powerful than unforgiveness.** Forgiveness is the light that raises you up into freedom. But unforgiveness will drag you down into darkness and lock you up in the chains of your hurt, your past and your regrets.

## THE FORGIVING HEART

Forgiveness is a *heart matter* so it clearly starts from the heart. **The act of forgiveness is not complete until you also *forget* the offence.** Just as our Father in Heaven loved us so much, He forgave us and blotted out all records of our sins which are no longer pinned against our names. He doesn't remember them anymore (**Jer. 31:34**). We are free of the stain of sin through the Blood of His Son Jesus Christ.

> *"For God so loved the world that He gave His only begotten Son, that whosoever believeth in Him should not perish, but have everlasting life.* [17] *For God sent not His Son into the world to condemn the world; but that the world through Him might be*

*saved."* (**John 3:16-17**)

God is Love and Forgiveness. It was out of God's great love for us that He forgave us. We learn here that the act of forgiveness grows from the roots of peace and faith which is grounded in the *soil of love* in our hearts (**Eph. 3:17-19**). **If we abide in God then we should also love and forgive like Him, because we are His children.** God has set an example for us to follow; He is a forgiving and loving God (**1 John 4:7**). Forgiveness then is also a fruit of the Spirit (**Eph. 5:9**) / (**Gal. 5:22**).

But unforgiveness is the fruit of offence, anger and bitterness. If you are slow to anger then you will learn grace and mercy. If you are driven by your anger then offence will be in your heart and cursing will be on your lips. Be warned: you will eat the fruit of your confession (**Prov. 18:20**). God's character reveals that He is slow to anger and full of mercy and grace (**Psa. 103:8**).

For those who are *slow to anger*, compassion will overtake their heart and bring them inner peace and joy. Soon after that they are able to forget the offence. This is the example God has set for us; He is full of compassion, forgiving the sins of many even unto the third and fourth generation. **The love of God also blossoms in forgiveness (Exod. 34:6-7).**

> *"If a man says, I love God, and hateth his brother, he is a liar: for he that loveth not his brother whom he hath seen, how can he love God whom he hath not seen?* [21] *And this commandment, have we from Him, that he who loveth God love his brother also."* (**1 John 4:20-21**)

# THE CHAINS OF BITTERNESS

There is more to forgiveness than mere words because it starts from the heart. **Every time you forgive you enter a new beginning** but unforgiveness cripples progress. For without forgiveness, there is no healing for the hurting soul. When you have been able to forgive, perfect love will be your reward and bring you wholeness. **The first step of forgiveness towards healing may be the scariest or unthinkable thing for you but it is the most important step you need to take to start the process of healing.** Your forgiving the offender will set you free from the bondage of bitterness.

It is foolishness to live and dwell on unforgiveness and bitterness; you will lose your friends as a result. Unforgiveness is like a snake. After it has bitten its victim, it will then turn to bite another. It won't stop because it is consumed by its own foolishness and in the attempt to protect itself; it swallows its own venom and is destroyed. **Unforgiveness is a friend to no one and will never be.** It has no respect for anyone regardless of who you are. It is a parasite of the soul that eats away at a good heart till there is nothing left of you. It is an invisible rock tied onto your chest, whose weight is unbearable until you release the unforgiveness in your heart. It is like bitter water unfit to drink. Its cruelty is like sharp arrows piercing the heart and making the bone sick with grief. **The bitterness of unforgiveness causes division and separates even the closest of friends.**

**Unforgiveness and animosity are terrible things because they separate you from experiencing the love of God.** You may see unforgiveness as a wall protecting you from those who have offended you but it is actually the other way around. Resentment has trapped and imprisoned you. If you are caught up in this bitter trail, unable to turn onto the right path, you are only killing yourself slowly by the pain and bitterness of unforgiveness in your heart. LET IT GO! Your life is worth more than the rage and destruction of hell. **When God created us, He didn't create us from the power of bitterness but from the power of love and wisdom.**

## THE BATTLE FOR YOUR HEART

Unforgiveness is like a fierce creature caged in; brutal in its attack and destructive in its blow. When you first release forgiveness from your heart the dark forces of unforgiveness and bitterness will be awakened to put up a desperate fight against you, in order to hold their ground. And just like a violent and aggressive beast, they will never go down without a fight. The *spirit of hate and bitterness* will try to make that decision of forgiveness difficult for you by reminding you of the hurt you went through, causing you to believe that it was better not to even think about it rather than to confront it and be faced with more bitterness.

In your confusion, the battle for your heart becomes intense and the decision of forgiveness retreats into oblivion leaving you to pickup the broken pieces again of disappointment and hurt. This is pride really working and it leaves no room for God to work. But have faith and press on through the process toward your healing; **the longer you stay immersed in the river of healing the cleaner you become**. If you keep on, when you finally push through the clouds you will see the sun and new strength and direction will come to you. You will soar with healing in your wings, and you will be free indeed.

Now, if ever you feel yourself drifting back into that old rotten place of unforgiveness immediately recognise it and confess your victory in God. Give no ground to that old serpent; for it is cunning and deceitful. Apply the ointment of forgiveness every day and every time you get the chance to do so. To achieve something you must take the first step towards it. This same truth is also found with healing. I urge you with all my heart that once you are free, endeavour to be free of the ungodly rage of unforgiveness and its chains of bitterness.

## FORGIVENESS AND PEACE

In an earlier Chapter, I spoke about the peacemaker. **One trait of the peacemaker is that he can initiate the process of forgiveness by giving and receiving forgiveness.** If you are unable to forgive those who have hurt you, you will not be able to experience peace until you become the peacemaker yourself.

In any argument, the true winner is the one who chooses to forgive by either giving forgiveness or asking for it. He is above his offender if he does this. He has won a far greater victory within by freeing his heart from bitterness and hate. **The fruit of peace is oneness of the heart and a sound mind**. Which is better to have; a broken heart filled with bitterness or a sound heart filled with peace? Why build unforgiveness in your heart because of a senseless argument that leads to division and destruction? Families are torn apart by unforgiveness and bitterness. But if you have the heart of God then you have the heart of the peacemaker.

God's favour and glory will flourish in him who possesses the heart of peace; for Christ is peace and forgiveness. He can help you overcome all fleshly wars and unfruitful divisions. He can direct you into the paths of life.

Walk in forgiveness and you walk in the victory of God. **The righteous pursues forgiveness and his peace will never be taken away from him.** The victory of the righteous is marked by God Himself, written and remembered in Heaven before His Holy angels. This is one of God's many crowns that He will give to those who have forgiven and found peace; yes, to those who have listened to the Voice of the Spirit and walked after peace and oneness with the Father of Glory. Blessed are those who forgive others, for their Father in Heaven shall also forgive them and will grant them the right to enter Heaven. He will lead them in the paths of righteousness, goodness and mercy and their days will be filled with joy and peace. God shall raise them up with strength and His Glory shall be their reward. God shall do all of these according to His good pleasure towards those who walk in His Love and Forgiveness. Amen!

## WHAT IF THE SEASON NEVER COMES

I once talked with a man who was quite bitter and unforgiving towards his siblings and parents. They were all in rivalry, one against another. With the intent to help him, I then asked, *"Why don't you forgive them and let the past go."*

However, he was headstrong and counted all the things they had done. This seemed to cause so much pain in him as he expressed his heart. He, knowing me as a devout Christian, decided he'd give me his piece of wisdom. He quoted from **Ecclesiastes 3:1 – 8,**

> *"To everything, there is a season and a time for every purpose under the sun. Therefore, there is a time to love and a time to hate, a time for war and a time for peace. There is also a time to*

*forgive and it will come when the time is right"*

When he said this, I felt moved by the Spirit of God and asked him, *"What if that time never comes? What if you never get to forgive?"*

This confronting question made him think perhaps for the first time about his heart attitude. I pressed on with another thought, *"Life is all about choices. Everyone is where they are because of the choices they made. You are here talking to me because you chose to be here. It doesn't matter what the outcome is, big or small, unimportant or significant, a choice was made for it. Love and hate, war and peace are choices as well. Forgiveness is a choice you can make right now?"*

I had his attention by this time. Driving the message home, I went on to say, *"If this is the case, then understand also that, a season cannot come unless there is a seed for it. A farmer can't have a harvest unless he first sows the seeds for that harvest. If forgiveness is a season, it requires a seed to be sown for it. Sowing a seed is as easy as planting it in the soil. Likewise, forgiveness is the seed you can plant to bring that season."*

I finished off by quoting **Galatians 6:7-8** *"Be not deceived; God is not mocked: for whatsoever a man sows, that shall he also reap. For he that sows to his flesh shall of the flesh reap corruption; but he that sows to the Spirit shall of the Spirit reap life everlasting.*

*And let us not be weary in well doing: for in due season we shall reap, if we faint not. As we have therefore opportunity, let us do good unto all men, especially unto them who are of the household of faith."*

Are you also like this man, stuck in a season of hate and bitterness? Have you been struggling with an issue for a long time and just don't know if you will ever be free of it? It is time for you to choose change. The power to choose is in your hands.

Don't play the blame game and be the victim. Be a victor! Choose life and peace. Know that when you blossom within, the harvest is ripe to manifest on the outside, and how glorious will be that harvest when you plant in abundance the seeds of peace, love and hope in the Spirit.

## THE HEALING BEGINS

There is no easy way to heal a wounded heart but through pure, gradual healing alone, assisted by proper *Holy Spirit* surgery, medication and care. God can heal you but you have to let him work on you.

**Forgiveness is like the ointment of healing to the wounded heart**. The more you apply this healing ointment the better and stronger you will feel and soon you are completely free. If you want healing and are tired of the bitterness that eats at you every day, you must boldly face the truth today and accept the only medicine of healing for your wounded heart; *forgiveness*. Yes, the offender lost your trust and hurt you. Sure it's not easy for you to forgive as you have faced too much pain already. But you can turn it all around today. Trusting the offender again may be impossible and incomprehensible, seeing that the pain is too unbearable but the process of forgiveness can restore all of that for you if you give God a chance. Yes, bitterness will grip your heart the hardest and make you feel sick inside but it will blow over like bad weather if you let God take care of it. May the LORD give you His strength to forgive those who have hurt you so that you also may be free to enjoy the blessings God has purposed to give you.

**Your *tomorrow* will never experience true healing if you still carry unforgiveness and bitterness today.** The weight will never get lighter unless you choose to take it off and put it down.

Let go of the weight of unforgiveness and bitterness. I encourage you to find the time to sit down and pray to God and ask Him to help you. This is your appointed time for healing and progress if you choose it with all your heart. *You don't have to carry that weight anymore.* God loves you and no one will take that right from you. You can freely choose His love and be free, or continue with the heavy chains of bitterness weighing on your heart.

If you profess to be a true believer in Christ; follow Christ's example of forgiveness and choose peace by His Spirit. God wants to heal you and He wants you to be free from the pain that you have carried. *Your healing is ready to break forth upon you like the morning sun if you are willing to let it all go into God's hands.* **God responds to the heart that is responsive and obedient to Him.**

I don't know about you but when my heart is in the place of total peace, I would not trade it for a cheap argument. **Bitterness will remind you of your losses but forgiveness will remind you of your victories.**

If you dwell on past hurts it means you still carry unforgiveness in your heart. Don't let its roots grow deep within you. Uproot it while it is still young and its roots fragile and you will not have to worry about it growing into a huge tree. **From the belly of unforgiveness comes all forms of hate that can destroy you.** I urge you by the Spirit of God to respond to God's call to you today to forgive those who have done you wrong. Let Him heal your heart and set you free. Don't wait till the sun sets on you. Or else, you may regret that the one whom you had resented was really the one you loved dearly but because of your pride, you could not let go of the offence. Take that courageous step to cross that river of unforgiveness because your blessings await you on the other side. In the very hour that you finally forgive all your offenders, you will feel that ungodly weight fall right off your back.

There is also one more important thing you need to do and that is to forgive yourself for all your mistakes. It's not worth carrying guilt and regret for another day or another mile. You are too valuable for your cause. Don't let bitterness cripple you but overcome its evil sting with the power of love and forgiveness flowing from the Cross of Jesus Christ.

If you are struggling to find a starting point toward forgiveness, one of the most powerful acts of forgiveness is the *washing of the feet* (**John 13:1-17**). I have seen many healed; where tears of healing have poured upon the feet and the hearts of those who have partaken of the blessing of the LORD's example. Even generational curses with their hurts and pains are washed away in this one act of humility, love and reconciliation.

## CLEANING THE DIRTY BUCKET

Imagine your heart like a bucket before the Throne of the LORD GOD. Now, forgiving someone is like trying to clean out that bucket, filled with the filth of unforgiveness, bitterness and hate. This is the unwanted garbage that gets thrown into it; the unpleasant and horrid things that we don't like to deal with.

The longer the dirt stays there it will begin to give off an awful smell and the stench itself will not be pleasing to the LORD and those around you. **No one likes bad smell. And evil stored in the heart is a spiritual bad smell.**

So, what can we do to clean out this unwanted filth? Well, what would you do if someone told you to clean your bucket out? Of course, you clean the bucket with water and a bit of detergent or soap. Now imagine that you began filling that bucket with clean, fast-flowing water to flush it out. The contents of the bucket would rise to the top and overflow out of the bucket. So that's what happens when you first begin the *process of forgiveness*. All that ugliness rises to the surface but doesn't stay there, if you keep on with the process, it will overflow out of the bucket. The more you flush the bucket the cleaner it will become. In the end, all you are left with is clean overflowing water. Now, add a bit of cleaning detergent to scrub it out and wash it clean and you now have a clean, fresh-smelling bucket before the LORD.

This metaphor is simple to understand. That's what happens when you put good things into your heart. Your confession of forgiveness and blessing cleanses you and sets you free from the filth of unforgiveness and bitterness. But if you hold onto your bitterness it is like filling the same bucket with more filth until it overflows with awful grime.

I hope that this parable helps you see what unforgiveness does to your heart and your life. Purge your heart clean today by setting it right before the LORD and ask Him to help you forgive those who have offended you.

## ETERNAL LIFE OR DEATH?

Count no one's sin and God will not count your sins. On the

day of Judgement when the time comes for the LORD to reward you, He will reward you according to all that you have done, and that includes how many times you were able to overcome and stood firm to the end. He will reward you for your forgiveness. Unforgiveness has no reward before the LORD and those who hold it in their heart miss out on the Father's blessing.

**The only reward of unforgiveness before the Throne of our God is the lake of eternal fire.** This sounds scary, but it is the truth. What is not useful in the Kingdom of God is thrown away in the fire to be burnt and destroyed. Jesus doesn't want us to be lost to the eternal lake of fire instead He wants us to share in the glorious love of God. He was able to forgive others on the Cross and laid His life down for us. The same Christ calls to our hearts to forgive and find victory in the finished work of His Cross and Resurrection. Don't miss out on the Father's love instead set yourself right before the LORD today and be free of the chains of unforgiveness. **If you love your life don't give into arrogance. Don't let pride control you and cause you to become bitter.**

**Unforgiveness is a killer of aspirations and a hindrance to your blessings.** Every choice in your heart determines what you reap in the future. Choose forgiveness today and be free. Choose God and choose Christ. But if you choose unforgiveness the call of hell is closer to you than Heaven. Now is your time to be free; this is your moment of truth and salvation. Christ freely gives eternal life to you. Receive it with all your heart and be free!

# CHAPTER 10

# THE POWER OF MEDITATING UPON GOD'S WORD

*"As for Me, this is My Covenant with them, saith the LORD; My Spirit that is upon thee, and My Words which I have put in thy mouth, shall not depart out of thy mouth, nor out of the mouth of thy seed, nor out of the mouth of thy seed's seed, saith the LORD, from henceforth and forever."* **Isaiah 59:21**

I wanted to close this book on a high note and get you going forward because I am for your blessing and salvation, and I know God wants to seriously prosper you and give you great success. Above all else, I want you to find Christ and make Him the Centre of your life; that's the starting point.

I learnt one truth as I put this book together with the help of the Holy Spirit. When the *Word of Wisdom* comes to uplift you and drive you forward, do not let it go—take hold of it before it passes you by. Write it down so you can remember it and meditate on it.

**The power and purpose of the Word cannot be tainted or affected by man; it is sent by God to change the cause of man.**

When I had finally reached the target number of pages for this book I then went into the process of editing which meant I had to go through the book again. Whilst in this process, I was greatly affected in my spirit by what I read. There was a change in my thinking and in my heart and the same words of wisdom from the pages of this book came alive and soaked me so much, my language was full of *faith declarations* and I felt good about it. Even my confidence grew for my own success and I felt the favour of God saturate the atmosphere. I also felt a new strength had been released from Heaven into my spirit. God's word was constantly before my eyes so much that this had a great impact on my heart.

If the words from this book have done something wonderful to me I am confident that they will also do something powerful to you when you take hold of the truth that lies in its pages, filled with God's wisdom and power. I encourage you to take it and apply it to your life. God's wisdom holds the keys to unlock every door of blessing. **Wisdom food will not only fill you up but make you fit for your success.**

I soaked the words in this book so much that when I awoke on the third day of editing I was so filled with inspiration I began to pray and faith rose out of me as I spoke words of blessing into my spirit and upon my life. Moreover, I began to reflect on the wisdom that came from the *Word of God* and all of a sudden the

*Spirit of Prophecy* came over me and I began to prophesy over my life and over the lives of my family. It was such a powerful experience. From doing this, I came to a greater understanding of the wonderful truth of meditating upon God's Word. The same exercise of meditating and focusing only on what one desires is exactly laid down in the same instructions given by God to the people of Israel through Joshua. This is what God said to Joshua in **Joshua 1:7-8**,

> *"Only be thou strong and very courageous, that thou mayest observe to do according to all the law, which Moses my servant commanded thee: turn not from it to the right hand or to the left, that thou mayest prosper whithersoever thou goest.* **8** ***This Book of the law shall not depart out of thy mouth; but thou shalt meditate therein day and night, that thou mayest observe to do according to all that is written therein: for then thou shalt make thy way prosperous, and then thou shalt have good success.***"

You can also find this in **Psalms 1**. If this book could have such an effect on me, how much more is the *Word of God* which is above every other book? Meditate upon (declare) the Word day and night until it takes hold of your being. The Body of Christ is powerless without the Word of Life.

Not a lot of people like reading, especially the Bible because it can be boring and monotonous but this is only a small sacrifice to pay for a *grand result* that could change the course of your own life. Take a hold of God's Word wholeheartedly and you will change your life forever. It is God's power for transformation and it is God's Key to the supernatural in Him. You see, **God's Word bends circumstances to fulfil its purpose because the authority of the Word is above all else (Isa. 55:11) / (Eph. 3:20).** How wonderful is the greatness of our God, Hallelujah!

LET THIS TRUTH BE EMBEDDED DEEP INTO YOUR SPIRIT SO THAT IT WILL BE LIKE FIRE IN YOUR BONES!

Please read on...

God blesses effort and diligence. Achievers are those who put their heart into anything they do and relentlessly pursue the outcomes they seek. *Achievement is the fruit of diligence.* Nothing compares to the fruit of diligence that comes from abiding in the Word of God. **Those who walk in the Word walk in superior favour.**

Put aside your excuse of laziness or tiredness, time constraints, or a 'not-for-me' attitude and get into the Word. **Make the Word your life and its power will become your life.** Faithfully digest the Word until it transforms you. **Proverbs 10:4** says,

*"He becometh poor that dealeth with a slack hand: but **the hand of the diligent maketh rich.**"*

Will you be diligent for your breakthrough, success, healing and prosperity? Then be diligent in the Word of God. **Proverbs 12:27** says,

*"The SUBSTANCE of the diligent man is precious."*

What you have in you is precious because you have the power to change your own life and bring about the blessing that you seek. You already possess what it takes to be successful but you just have to be diligent and discover this precious gift in you. In addition, God's Word can help you discover that precious gift and empower you with Heavenly firepower to overcome and be the master of your ordained destiny. The precious Word of God is the power of the Highest. **Proverbs 13:24** says,

*"The soul of the sluggard desireth, and hath nothing: but **the soul of the diligent shall be made fat.**"*

Are you tired of searching for answers because you are so hungry for change? Look no further my friend for **the power to change is yours through the Word of God, and the *fatness of your blessing* is within your grasp by obeying the Words of the Spirit.** Take hold of the power of the Word of God right now and meditate upon it until it overflows out of you. Be diligent and you will be filled. God's Word can do anything for you if you walk with it faithfully. This is not man's wisdom; it is God's and with it is supernatural power. It matters to God if you are diligent in His Word. If you walk in the Word you already have an advantage above the rest because those who walk in the power of the Holy Spirit are those who have been consuming the Word of God assiduously. Out of your diligence could come a grand idea and plan that could change your life forever, and above that, God becomes manifest in your life.

The Hebrew definition of the word 'meditate' means to mutter or speak *Words of blessing* under your breath *constantly*. **If you are always thinking and talking about problems then you'll have more of it heaped on you.** But God wants you to talk about the solutions; speak His Words of blessing and I guarantee you a hundred percent, you will be satisfied with the fruit of your mouth. **Proverbs 21:5** says,

> *"**The thoughts of the diligent tend only to plenteousness**; but of everyone that is hasty only to want (or poverty)."*

Are you hasty about just getting through your Bible reading for the day? You need to do better than that if you want your blessing. It has to come from your heart. **One of the biggest killers of quality is complacency.** To seek after quality is to pursue the finer details of brilliance. There is no higher splendour than God's presence and no greater quality than the absolute purity of God's Word. Are you willing to spend a day with God? One day spent in the presence of the LORD is better than a thousand days elsewhere because it is one day spent with the King of kings and the LORD of lords.

It is one day spent with the LORD GOD of GLORY, POWER and MAJESTY, the Creator of Heaven and Earth.

Jesus Christ our LORD knew the power of the Word. He is the Word and when He was here on Earth He walked in the power of the Word (**Acts 10:38**).

He told the devil off in his face with this truth that, *"Man shall not live by bread alone but by every Word that proceeds out of the mouth of God."* **Whatever leaves God's mouth never returns to Him empty but always accomplishes the purpose that God sends it to achieve.** God's Word will not fail to prosper (**Isa. 55:11**). So you can be sure that when you meditate on His Word and let it take hold of you, it will change the way you think and the way you live. It will bring about the prosperity that God wants for you because God doesn't go halfway with His Word, He goes all the way to fulfil the promise He declared to you. He is our Father who takes pleasure in the prosperity of His Children.

**Proverbs 22:29** says,

*"Seest thou a man diligent in his business? He shall stand before kings; he shall not stand before MEAN MEN."*

So if you are diligent with wisdom you will *stand before* great men because the might of great men also lie in the purposes of God.

The Words, *stand before,* in this verse mean the doors of opportunity will open for you because you unlock them by your diligence in applying God's Wisdom not only found in this book but in the ultimate Book of books, the Bible, the *WORD OF GOD, the WORD OF GLORY. It is the Book of the VOICE OF WISDOM CALLING OUT TO YOU.*

If your blessing and breakthrough mean so much to you, then grab a hold of the answer that lies in the wisdom I have been pouring out to you, from the Word of God and the Spirit of God. If you care enough about your success and prosperity, then God's Book should not just be another ordinary book in your hand, it should be the book that transforms you daily into God's glory. Take hold of its power by meditating upon it till it soaks you and until you produce the results promised by God (**John 15:8, 16**).

But if you are not diligent, think about the idea of standing before *mean men.* The Words, 'mean men,' are talking about negative opportunities, and negative people, especially the ones you detest. In other words, if you are wondering why you keep ending up with more problems or sitting amongst the wrong crowd, it is because of your slack and lazy attitude towards God's wisdom and perhaps your disobedience to the *Voice of His Spirit.*

Be diligent about wisdom and she will be diligent and faithful to bring you before the doors of your *ordained* opportunities. God's Wisdom is not *fake decoration,* it is *faith declaration.* **Do not display God's Word on the Shelf instead display it in your life.** The best way to use God's gift in you is through the Word of God. Your gift can only be cultivated in diligence.

"*A* <u>*man's gift*</u> *maketh room for him, and bringeth him before great men."* (**Prov. 18:16**)

A man's gift will unveil his opportunities, reputation and his reward. In a man's gift lies his opportunity to be successful and it points him to his wealth. Embrace the gift in you for it will be your best friend for the rest of your life. Because your gift comes from God steward it well and it will make great. If you are faithful and diligent with your gift, then God will provide a greater platform for you to display what you have to offer.

My dear beloveds, in concluding this Chapter, and this Book, God doesn't want us to neglect the power and the gift that is in us which was given by the Holy Spirit. God wants us to meditate on His Word and give ourselves wholly to it because it is our salvation and our blessing; the key to our prosperity and success (**1 Tim. 4:14-15**).

May these prophetic Words be true for you just as they were for Christ, *"For this cause came I unto this hour."*

I pray that you will find your true calling and purpose in life and if you haven't yet, then now is your chance for change. Run the race of faith with all your heart. Pursue the knowledge of Christ and teach the ways of God just as His Spirit has taught you to walk in Him. Be the light to the world and let the light of God shine brightly through you.

I prophesy that you are marked for an overflow of the heavenly blessings. Begin your journey right now and **take a hold of God's Word with all your heart. It is your guiding light to the Father's heart.**

Your breakthrough is at hand and so is your healing because Christ has already paid the full price for it on the Cross. For those who choose Christ, you are highly favoured by the LORD GOD.

I prophesy **Malachi 3:10** upon your life, that the LORD *will open up the windows of Heaven and pour you out a blessing that there shall not be enough room to receive it.* It is time for you to cross your own Jordan and possess the land of milk and honey which the LORD gives to you today (**Josh. 1:11**).

I pray you will choose Christ. I pray you will choose to be a blessing by being in the presence of the Almighty God always. Be a bright light by carrying your cross faithfully. Be a child of God by using His Wisdom to overcome your darkest fears and walk in the faith, hope and love of God. Be the best that you are because God gave you nothing but the best. Blessed are those who seek the will of God with all their hearts for they will be favoured highly by the Father in Heaven. Blessed are those who hear the Voice of the Spirit; the Voice of Wisdom calling out to every one of us today; calling us to *Obedience and Glory*.

Freely you have received the love and wisdom of God. I charge you now by the Will of God and by His Spirit in me. Go as the vessels of Christ and freely give to all those whom the LORD brings across your path. Be courageous and make a difference in a world that needs the healing touch of God flowing from your heart.

To God be all glory, honour and power forever, AMEN!!!

## CLOSING SCRIPTURE:
"Beloved, I wish above all things that THOU MAYEST PROSPER AND BE IN HEALTH, EVEN AS THY SOUL PROSPERETH... [4] I have no greater joy than to hear that MY CHILDREN WALK IN TRUTH... [11] Beloved, follow not that which is evil, but that which is good. He that doeth good is of God: but he that doeth evil hath not seen God."

**(3 John1:2, 4, 11)**

# I AM HOME AT LAST (POEM)

Once I have written for you, Shall I write again?
Be it a tale that adventure should unveil? Or a twist in my fading glory?
This earthen vessel Yet with sincerity, I grasp this life-giving water:
A fountain of youth it is. From the wells of wisdom and wonder springs forth inspiration. Oh inspiration. To my mellow self, it is but a true friend;
Never denying, never backing away
While I was yet formed in my mother's womb, inspiration stood to welcome me into this world. A sense of unpredictable destruction preyed in the unseen hour to consume me: An element sort my annihilation.
But inspiration was ordained to stand by me and destiny voiced her decree, "The warrior has come by the Spirit Untouched for Heaven's purpose"
I was sent unknown to myself. Yet within me, a call so great drew my heart to its cause. Like Jesus, I uttered those momentous words firmly, "For this cause came I unto this hour".
Beauty beheld me, while yet my frame was formed. Beauty beheld me.
When time nodded, I came forth and laughter and joyful tears filled the air.
Was it shepherds who waited for my appearing? Did wise men seek out my tender soul? Yet purity from Heaven left its glory on me as I embarked on this journey. Earth being my valley and Heaven being my King's table: I set my course upon the King of all kings. My blissful self then discovers His passion. I go forth and become all that He has written about me. Destiny is my decree and my guard.
Oh Destiny, the seal upon my life. Oh Destiny, the Father's love unfeigned
Then shall my race end and Honour unmatched shall welcome me home.
When I have finally accomplished all that He has sent me to do. His Anointing was my Ordination. Now it has become my Crown.
My Father opens His Arms and embraces me I am home at last...I am home at last.

*Norma — Sabadi (Sunday 29-11-2015)*

# About the Author

Norman, and his wife, Olivia are the Senior Pastors of *"The Place Where He Speaks,"* based in Rockhampton, Queensland, Australia. Marked with the Fire of God, Norman began his journey with the Lord in 1999.

In following the humble efforts of the prophets and apostles, they, by the help of the Holy Spirit, ensured to document their *Commissioning Moment with God*— Norman has also done the same here for the benefit of the reader:

> Then Jesus said, "Norman[1]...God Calls you and Anoints you to reach the nations with the Word of God. Preach His Gospel of Peace and Power." Jesus then took three large jars

which were filled with Anointing Oil and He poured all the Oil from the jars upon Norman to anoint him as the Carrier, Leader and Servant of The Great Mandate of Revival (the Great Awakening of God)—19 February 2002.

Through many years of nurturing and mentorship under the Holy Spirit, the appointed time has come for the Glory Mandate to be fulfilled, and to accomplish the call of mentoring God's people into the Great Revival Fire. For the Glory of the Lord is ready to be manifested to the world, for the shaking of the nations.

Endnote:
1 (Sabadi N.M.T. 2023. Chapter 10 - The Great Induction and Anointing Service, *Chosen to Carry the Glory - Carry the Fire of Jesus,* Norman Sabadi Publishing, Rockhampton, Queensland, Australia pp.165-207).

# Chosen

## CHOSEN TO CARRY THE GLORY-CARRY THE FIRE OF JESUS

YOU CAN SUPPORT THE MINISTRY AND WORK OF PASTOR NORMAN BY:

* WRITING A REVIEW ON THIS BOOK AND SHARE SNIPPETS OF YOUR BOOKMARKS ON SOCIAL MEDIA
* BUY THIS BOOK AS A GIFT FOR SOMEONE.
* SHARING THE MESSAGE OF THIS BOOK WITH OTHERS.

**DONATE TO**

**PAYPAL:**
https://www.paypal.com/paypalme/normsabadi

*Thank you so much for your support and may the Lord bless you abundantly*

# Media

**Facebook The Place Where He Speaks Group Page:**
https://www.facebook.com/groups/652589851978873/

**YouTube Channel: The Place Where He Speaks**
https://www.youtube.com/channel/UCqjypOfptKjmYNVB0_2I2wA

**YouTube Handle:**
@theplacewherehespeaks

**Norman Sabadi — Facebook Profile**
https://www.facebook.com/nsabadi

**Norman Sabadi — Youtube Channel**
https://www.youtube.com/channel/UC0OHqOX1OyciINWAhpLUJ9A

**Youtube Handle:**
@normansabadi

# Contact Details

We would love to hear from you, about testimonies, praise reports, prayer requests and preaching requests also, or any other thing the Lord has impressed upon you to share. You can reach Pastor Norman through the following methods:

**Personal email:** normansabadi@ymail.com

**THE PLACE WHERE HE SPEAKS**
**Email:** theplacewherehespeaks@gmail.com

www.ingramcontent.com/pod-product-compliance
Lightning Source LLC
Chambersburg PA
CBHW051929160426
43198CB00012B/2087